A Journey of
Significance:
Albert Diepeveen

God is good! ALWAYS!)

I THES. 5:18

Written by Greg Yates

Overcoming 10 Common Leadership Fears: How to Turn Common Fear into Your Uncommon Breakthrough (2017)

The Breakthrough: A Business Fable About Getting on the Same Page to Get Results That Stick (2017)

Broken: How Being Broken Unlocked the Greatest Success of My Life (2016)

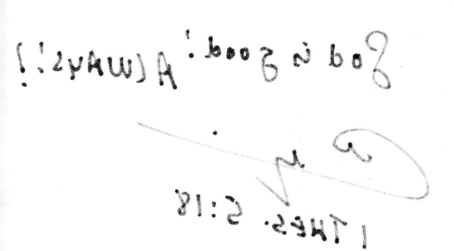

2

A Journey of Significance:
Albert Diepeveen

Business on Purpose

Written by Greg Yates

A Journey of Significance: Albert Diepeveen (Business on Purpose)

ISBN-10: 1723006033

ISBN-13: 978-1723006036

"Albert's part in bringing Youth for Christ to the area, and Theresa bringing hospice to our town, changed the area forever. Albert's personal philosophy impacted our lives and our financial acuity to better line up with God's teachings."

Pastor Vern and Linda Smith

= = = = =

"This book describes Bert perfectly. Bert, in essence, is 'loyalty.' Two Bert quotes which stand out for me are, 'You cannot out-give God,' and 'God is good, always.'"

Peter Briscoe, former President of EuroPartners

= = = = =

"The amazing story of how Jesus delivered a 40+ year old entrepreneur to live the abundant Spirit-filled life of inexpressible joy and transgenerational impact. This biography will encourage anyone to take more risks for God."

Christopher P. Bray, JD, CPA
Managing Partner at Christopher P. Bray Associates, LLC

= = = = =

"I had the privilege of having Albert in Belfast about 25 years ago. He gave a presentation of 'Business by the Book' to CBMC members. With special memories, I commend this Journey of Significance. May God bless all who absorb its message."

Jim Johnston, Former CBMC International and Euro-Partners Member

= = = = =

"Many are happy being followers of Christ, so long as it doesn't cost too much. In the midst of severe challenges, Albert lives a life of simple faith and profound influence. Read this book and walk with the Lord on your own path to being simply profound."

Ken Korkow, former marine leading great marketplace ministry to the military in Nebraska and South Dakota

= = = = = =

"*A Journey of Significance* wonderfully captures the life story of Albert Diepeveen. In the words of the great Dutch Prime Minister, Abraham Kuyper, 'There is not a square inch in the whole domain of our human existence, over which Christ, who is sovereign over all, does not cry out, Mine!'"

Bob Milligan, Founder and former Chairman & CEO of M.I. Industries; former President and Chairman of CBMC International; former Chairman of the U. S. Chamber of Commerce

= = = = = =

"Albert has been a spiritual guide and positive influence in my life. His slogan is, 'God is GOOD… always!' The work Albert did with CBMC and through biblical financial teachings has been a blessing to many around the world. I know this book will bless all who read it."

A Canadian friend and successful businessman, Andy Weststeyn

= = = = = =

"You will be inspired and blessed by this book. Albert's intriguing stories will leave you wanting more. This book reminds me that we all leave an impact and the possibilities are unlimited when we live in the promises of God."

Tom Cunnington, Circuit Court Judge

= = = = = =

"My wife and I have been impacted by the Lord working in Albert's life and witnessing his commitment to live by the biblical standards he teaches. He is a man of God, governed by the word of God, and demonstrates that 'God never gives us a principle that we cannot live with because God never lies, and He can always be trusted.'"

Don Mitchell, retired Executive Director of Quality for General Motors North American Operations

= = = = = =

"In the world of business, real Christians are rare. I was often surprised to find that there are people who are spiritually empty. Although most cannot meet Albert in person, I am so glad that somebody took time to paint a picture of him. This has become a wonderful and encouraging picture."

Siegfried Buchholz, former Director of the American BASF Group, and General Director of the Austrian BASF Group

= = = = = =

"I believe this book is powerful and has the potential to make people search their hearts and challenge their relationship between God and their core values. The story of Albert Diepeveen is a living example of what God can do through a man who makes himself available to the Creator. If you are ready and willing to be challenged, enriched and impacted, this book is for you."

John Hines, Pastor at Cornerstone Church and YFC Director at Manteno High School

= = = = = = =

"Albert has trusted God and found Him to be true, real, loving, and above all else, faithful in fulfilling His promises. Albert has always encouraged me to trust God in all things, especially in business and money management."

Milton J. Smit, M.D

= = = = = = =

"God will design a path for your life, which will lead to a personal relationship with the Lord. This well-written book can show you how God works, and you can become a true disciple of the Lord using Albert's experience and his spiritual principles in your personal journey with God."

W.C. Hultman, former top GE Executive

= = = = = = =

"Albert Diepeveen has been used by God to influence literally thousands of young lives for the sake of the

Gospel. Albert's long-standing visionary leadership with the board at Youth for Christ has spanned more than three decades. Since helping to launch the initial work in 1982, Albert has been instrumental in growing the vision to include the Chicago metropolitan region. Albert lives out the great commission in very tangible ways. His spiritual influence on my own life has been immeasurable."

Rick Selk, CEO of Youth for Christ Chicago

This book is dedicated to the men and women who have accepted the CALLING of *Business on Purpose* and are brave enough to test God's promises.

Foreword

Being asked to share my story was a great struggle for me. I am just a man who has been blessed with the opportunity to depend on God through the difficulties of life and the reality of suffering. If I have anything worth sharing it is because I have learned to depend on a loving God who will not give us a principle we cannot implement. I have tried my best to be clay in the hands of Almighty God.

Please don't imagine I am stronger than you are. This book is not about me, rather the significance of a journey where our steps are established by our Loving Father (Proverbs 16:9) and we each have opportunity to choose dependence on Him. This truth has influenced my life and allowed me to influence others. My prayer for this book is that you take my experiences and place yourself in the awesome plan you were created to fulfill. Follow God's principles of abundance and help others experience all they were created to enjoy.

I hope you will see the possibilities that exist in your life and your business through this humble story. God is good. Always. Hang in there.

Albert Diepeveen

Author's Perspective

How do you write about a man who doesn't want to be written about? This has been a prominent topic of discussion in my many conversations with Albert--a paradox so real it has woven its way into the story itself. In fact, it is the story.

When God genuinely works, man is struck by awe as he becomes aware of his own minuscule part in the story. Yet, the story itself serves not to glorify the creation, but the Creator. No matter what I try to say in disclaimer here, Albert will categorically respond in his unworthiness to be listed among God's champions. Alas, here we are.

My own story is much easier to tell. I got it wrong and God intervened. I take no credit; I find no human satisfaction, only despair in my failures. But what if I did 'get it right'? What if I walked the path of the Lord for a generation, and yet was so dramatically aware of my inadequacy it horrified me to consider the possibility of a beacon shining on my life. As if I were a model. As if I were perfect.

Is obscurity inherently more righteous than public humility? Is it possible to give God glory while we tell our own stories, with the focus on us? Is it possible to do both?

With the biblical story of King David as my case study, I say yes! It must be so, or we wage a war with no heroes, no examples, no witnesses to the truth of our God. If it isn't possible to tell the stories of men used by God, we must discount the Holy Spirit inspired writings of Hebrews 11 and the great cloud of witnesses! I believe God is still demonstrating His power, superimposed on our lives through the image of Christ by His divine plan. That is a story always worth telling; a story we are compelled to share.

Albert has become a mentor to me. This wasn't by his design, but by our interaction in situations neither of us planned. Albert has 'leavened' the world around him with the salt of the earth and the light of the world. When I think of Albert, I don't think of his talents or abilities (which are diverse and many). I don't think of a powerful speaker, writer or any such human traits. I think of his simple words. I think of his quiet spirit. I know that long ago Albert disappeared into the arms of Grace, and his life on earth provides a window to the cross of Christ. His words quietly and persistently reflect the scripture and rarely anything more. His unassuming reminder is positioned by the Spirit of God, who is the author and finisher of our faith.

I don't tell this story to lift you up, Albert. Hear me, brother. I am telling the story of God at work in the life of a man who simply chose to let him. I ponder and share the simple decisions you've made and remained committed to. I share the surrender of pain and the realization of true prosperity. I share all of this knowing that your light has remained on the hilltop for all to see, not as much a lighthouse as a warming fire for the stranger who is suffering in the darkness.

This is a chapter in the glorious story of Jehovah, our great and mighty deliverer. His Word will endure forever.

The Interview – Introduction

He sits across from me, legs crossed. He has a faraway look on his face as he sips his coffee. It's a familiar scene after these months of conversations, but still fresh. He has decided he likes the view from my chair better--I suppose because after a few occasions on the back deck of my home he has gravitated there. I am honored.

A head full of gray hair, he still looks much younger than his years. He seems more like a friend than a mentor. About twenty-five years my senior, he has settled in to my life like a comfortable companion. I'm learning that that is just Albert's way.

"I just trust God. Once I made a commitment to him, I wasn't gonna break my word."

Albert's thick Dutch accent still hung in the air as I thought about those words just now. In fact, I'm still thinking about them. After all of the steps I've taken in life and business, these words seemed to sum up the answer to a hundred questions.

I wonder if Albert actually thinks differently about that statement than most of us, or if it just seemed that way to me. We make promises and commitments to God all our lives, and if we break them we know God will forgive us. Suddenly my brain was tingling with the possibility that in a simple phrase, Albert had perhaps voiced the most significant characteristic about his relationship with God. He didn't say he was perfect or without sin. He sipped his coffee and had just told me that the promise he made to God wasn't taken lightly. Once he said it, he was bound to keep it as any good Dutchman would do.

Looking for clues with Albert will always lie in the simple things. He's not a complex man. More than anyone I have ever met, he sees himself as the clumsiest person in the room. He genuinely can't imagine why he is treated with such regard.

It's important to understand this perspective or Albert's story won't be interpreted properly. The dynamic of Albert's simplicity, and how he views himself as insignificant, is as organic as nature and that isn't typically why these stories get written. My task in sharing what I have learned is a daunting one because it treads delicately on the sensibilities of the reader.

Clumsy. Yes, I did use that word. It was the only word I could deal to you when I looked through the deck. Albert simply can't imagine why anyone would want to hear his story. He doesn't feel he's done anything at all. He made choices, lived them out and trusted God. It's uncommon to accomplish what Albert has, but he doesn't seem to see it that way. He's just done what he said he would do, and people are amazed by that. I find myself adopting his mindset when we are together, which forms a glaring contrast to the bulk of my own life.

"Once I made that commitment to God, I wasn't gonna break my word." From that foundation, more commitments were made; ones that became flesh on the bones of an otherwise theoretical structure of faith. Albert's faith balanced every equation of his life for the last forty years.

Annoyingly Simple

In a world where we're taught that being 'different' is critical to success, Albert built the ark. That's how I see it, anyway. Streamlined, indestructible and always top-side-up because it is built based on the instructions of God himself. Apparently remaining afloat for the long haul is more important than being sleek, fast or next generation.

It was a long time before I could relate to Albert's perspective. My thoughts toward him started out as 'naïve' and gradually trended toward 'consistent.' I always valued flexibility, creativity and speed in business, but Albert seemed stuck in firm constants. I was fixated on making the deal and Albert questioned whether the deal would, in any way, compromise the principles God had laid out. It seemed backward to me.

Can we really live in such Godly confidence that our only definition of success is remaining dead center in the path of God's will?

Does the Bible, with its ancient principles, provide the passageway to a successful life?

Can we actually trust what we cannot see?

These are hard questions and not to be rewarded with token answers. Before we relay an appropriately churchy answer, let's examine the experiences of a man who has put God's principles to the test and has the credentials to moderate a debate that goes on in the life of every Christian businessperson.

I can't wait to share it.

Chapter 1 – Telling the Story

It's easier to look back than it is to look forward. Life is full of twists and turns. In retrospect, we see how those twists and turns intersected life's most important components, even when we tried to steer away from them.

Why do we try to avoid the most important issues? Why do we fail to see how vital they are, even when they were right in front of us? They are hard. They are painful. Often, they are confusing and generally we never understand.

What if the consuming struggle of our lives stems primarily from our incessant need to understand things and to control them? Why do we have this desperate desire to steer the ship? Our perspective is too small. Our vision is too short. Come with me on a journey into simple, biblical truth from a man who calls himself a "dumb Dutchman."

An Unlikely Teacher

Albert has an uncanny way of sneaking up on you. That's one of the things that makes his story so much fun. He's that friend you know will tell you the truth, even when it's hard. You can't spend more than a few minutes with Albert without hearing this proclamation:

"God never gives us principles we can't implement, and He never asks us to do something that isn't for our good. As long as I embrace those premises, I'm confident in what will come as a result."

During our passionate interview sessions, I remember asking Albert if he always knew God had a special plan for his life. I was surprised by his answer.

"I'm not sure why God has used my life, to be honest." Albert looked into the distance as he continued. "I don't know why my voice is so important. Over time, you'd think my broken English would have become perfect, but it's not. I haven't done anything that will go down in the history books. I guess my life wasn't built for that; it was built to withstand the fire of being tested, and to store treasures where they will never be corrupted, and where thieves can never break in and steal."

Very few people will understand the riches of Albert's life. He didn't always make the decisions in business that would put himself, his profits, or his personal security first. His idea of sound business decisions meant making decisions that would reflect God's ownership of his business. He possesses an annoying vigilance, defending against anything that would fail to honor the biblical plans of God's word. Albert believes his resources are destined for purposes beyond human understanding. He doesn't possess the need to understand. Albert's greatest accomplishments are simple: to please God and love His people. He's found life's deepest satisfaction there. How do I know? Still, to this day, he has no regrets.

It's just my observation, but I don't think there was a step toward leadership that Albert ever really planned to take. I don't mean to say that he wasn't making plans, but Albert never saw himself as a businessman. In his own words:

"My success was as much a surprise to me as anybody."

Trying to tell Albert's story is like watching a school of fish swimming in the ocean. You can't see why they change direction, but when they do it is in perfect harmony. You can't see what they are pursuing or what is pursuing them. All you know is that regardless of their frantic motions, it is beautiful to watch.

Albert's life is filled with circumstances he never chose. It's full of pain he didn't deserve and discoveries he couldn't have imagined. In his own words, Albert sums it up: "I don't know why I am still alive, but I can't wait to see what is ahead of me. I don't know how a poor, sickly boy could have found the greatest wealth and strength in all creation."

Let's step into the stories that Albert has shared with me.

In All Things

Walking along the road in the early morning light, his mind wandered. "What do you have for me today, Lord? How can I glorify you today?"

Albert's day began much as it always had for the past forty years, searching every experience and every circumstance so he could be thankful for it specifically. Not just the good things, not just the obvious. His favorite were the ones that were open-ended; the ones God hadn't resolved yet. These were the ones that gave purpose to life, and he had learned to relish their potential.

"I know you never give me anything that isn't for my good and your glory, God, so thank you for this struggle with my back. I can't wait to see how you will use it for your purpose. Help me not to miss it. Help me not to let it overwhelm my senses so that I fail to see what you are doing. I know all of these things are going to be good. I can't wait!"

"Help me to tell others what you are doing in my life--not just in the past, but today.

"Thank you for allowing me to get older so I can see the beautiful pictures you have painted in my life.

"I couldn't see them when I was too close to them, but I see them now. I can't wait to be amazed by the ones that are still in progress, but I am too close to see. I just thank you for them anyway."

Being in his eighties had its benefits and its curses. He couldn't remember every name like he used to, and he spent an inordinate amount of time with physical challenges that come when we are beyond the deceptions of youth. He didn't mind slowing down but being unable to travel and teach as he desired challenged Albert's driving sense of purpose.

As he enjoyed this morning walk, his mind strummed over the memories of a very well-seasoned past. He never imagined he would live this long or participate in so much. Life itself had defined his story, woven with circumstances he would never have chosen for himself. How had satisfaction been so integral when there was an abundance of frustration and uncertainty? He smiled as he mouthed his patented answer instinctively: "I will give you thanks, Lord, in all circumstances," and he walked on.

Memories

"Look mama, they're dropping eggs!" Albert's ran and jumped with the bounce of a three-year-old. In a moment he was there again, the sights of unthinkable madness forcing their way into the history books. His mother, Fetje, shielded her eyes. Her heart pounded in speechless unison with her neighbor as their conversation was choked by the presence of paratroopers. The sky filled with them as a nation woke from the hope that they could avoid participation in another World War. The Netherlands had managed to stay neutral in World War I, but today that was not going to happen. The Hague was central to government and the ports of Holland were far too valuable for the Germans to forego.

Albert felt his mother's fear as she rushed him into the house. Their neighborhood of row houses had been a source of security and community. School, church and mutual support had provided a consistent lifestyle for the lower income families. It was all Albert had ever known. They walked to their church-based school; church was the center of their lives. As a toddler, Albert lived a life of adventure about the carefully constructed community, exploring and pretending without a care in the world. This day, however, that security was lost. Albert couldn't understand what was happening. He soon would.

The Dutch army fought the invasion for four days before the Germans started bombing the center of Rotterdam. With that, the Dutch army gave up the fight; they were no match for their invaders. For four days, Albert's family was sequestered in the small living room of their home, terrified to be seen through the window, let alone to leave the house. They could hear soldiers outside their home. The noise of gunshots and shouting terrified Albert and his sister. At one point, they had even seen German soldiers in front of their home and Dutch soldiers behind it. They prayed the soldiers wouldn't see each other and catch their home in the crossfire.

In one vivid instance, Albert crept carefully from the living room to use the toilet. Looking through the crack in the door, he saw two German soldiers staring into the window, looking for any sign of life. The image of the soldiers in their helmets, grenades strapped to their chests in full assault gear, would stick with Albert forever. His heart seemed to stop as he waited for them to move on. Eventually they lost interest and moved down the street. Albert's family were prisoners in their home, paralyzed by fear that would bind Albert to a sense of captivity for years to come.

Albert's father, Dirk Diepeveen, was on his way to work when the invasion began. He was rounded up by soldiers and locked in a storage building, along with many others. The Germans armed the door with explosives, so they wouldn't leave, but Albert's father climbed out the window so he could get to work.

Driven by duty, Albert's father knew that this day would be a critical day for the patients he served in the mental hospital. They wouldn't understand what was happening. It was common knowledge that the Germans had an intense hatred for the Jews, but very soon the occupied population learned that the handicapped and mentally ill were despised as well.

Eventually, the Germans converted the hospital into a military facility and forced the patients and workers out. It was only the beginning of the oppression and brutality to be experienced by a victimized people and their huddled families. Albert's family was pulled apart and given no control over their fate.

The vivid memories continue to assault Albert's thoughts, even as the boy exists inside the man.

Comprehending the Past

Watching Albert's eyes as the memories unfold captures my imagination. Personal memories that have become the legend of history flow from a man who intuitively sees it for what it is. It's his own window into unfolding momentum which changed the world. To hear him tell it, I know the momentum has never stopped.

From an early age, Albert's entire life revolved around the church and scripture. Deeply embedded into his thought processes, the words had become rote. But in this nightmare of war, ritual toward an abundant God paled to a growing search for food and a lack of resources, which soon redefined life for his struggling family.

Comprehending the past would play a powerful role in Albert's belief of the future. His view of God and of himself began to be shaped through circumstances beyond his control. There was no turning back.

Chapter 2 – The Occupation

Was today so much different than other days? His curiosity grew as he heard the whispering voices of his parents. Why was it so loud outside and why were people running? Why couldn't he go out and play?

Albert's father worked nearby in a hospital for people who were considered mentally ill. Albert didn't know what that meant, just that his father was an important man and well respected. Albert had never seen him with fear in his eyes until now.

War seemed as normal as any of Albert's childhood memories. Even before the occupation, Albert's family was very poor, unbeknownst to Albert. Their neighborhood provided its own circle of friends, school and church. Albert learned of God early and his parents lived a life of service.

Albert and his mother, 1936.

Albert knew there was a God and he believed that God was angry with them, for some reason. He never understood why.

May of 1940 was the beginning of an occupation and Albert's first real memories were founded on it. The challenges of life, the very reality of life, was now based on oppression and subjection to denial of basic freedoms. As a child, he became almost invisible to the world as he absorbed the images of the occupation by Nazi forces. This was their new normal and Albert, the child, was learning to survive in the midst of it.

Watching airplanes dogfight in the sky was a sporting event for the boys. Closer to home, the death and abuse brought by the Nazis became far too common. Albert pretended not to see or to care. He had learned to walk the other direction when he saw soldiers. Once, he even saw a man killed and his home blown up so that everyone knew they could not resist their captors. Albert found himself wondering why this evil was destroying their lives. Even as a boy, he believed that God was punishing them.

Albert was the youngest of four. Childhood had been interrupted, but the boy inside him made the war almost tolerable. It was the only life he had ever known. Resources were limited and almost entirely consumed by the Germans as they raided the possessions of local families. In many cases, families were thrown out of their homes to make room for soldiers. They were given two hours to gather whatever they could carry.

Early in the occupation, much of life seemed normal, but gradually broke down as time elapsed. This became especially evident as the war went badly for Germany. Living in hunger was the norm as food became scarce. Albert's mother ate very little so her children could be fed to satisfaction. He watched as once proud people stood in line for food, often with pieces of wood tied to their feet because they had no shoes. All copper and brass had to be surrendered, then all blankets and bicycles. Without bicycles, transportation for the average person was nearly impossible.

Soap was also scarce, but rarely was it mentioned as the need for food and other basics was far more critical. In a group of people, you'd be bound to find someone covered in lice.

The Christian mental hospital where Albert's father worked was two miles from their home. The hospital was evacuated to make room for a base from which the Nazis would launch V1 and V2 missiles toward England. Another launch site was built in the woods a short distance from Albert's home. The rockets were overwhelming as their deafening sound ripped through the half mile into Albert's bedroom, day and night. Even worse were the failed launches that kept everyone in fear as they fell into the surrounding area.

When the Germans began launching rockets, the technology was far from perfect. Once the launch sites were identified, the allies' attempts to knock them out devastated the local city and surrounding area. Most of the destruction and death was brought on the local population.

In 1944 when the mental hospital was evacuated, Albert's father accompanied patients to care for them. He wasn't to return until 1947, leaving Albert's mother to care for their four children on her own. The family was torn apart by war, but an even more extreme trial would be levied on Albert.

In February of 1945, the bombing around The Hague where Albert lived had become so intense, and food was so scarce, that Albert's mother decided they had to leave their home. They had no idea if they'd be able to reconnect with Albert's father, nor did they know if he was even still alive.

Albert's older brothers, Broer and Dirk, had left in December of 1944 with hopes of reaching relatives more than 150 miles away. It was a long time before they received word that the boys had arrived safely. Dirk caught a rabbit and sent it with a man on a bike who was traveling to The Hague, with instructions to deliver it to his mother. Albert smiles with the memory of the man riding up, the rabbit hanging from his bike. It was the first meat they'd had in months.

Albert, his mother, and his sister slept in the same bed for warmth until they found the means for a journey out of The Hague. In order to travel anywhere in the Netherlands, you had to cross many bridges. Much of the land was below sea level and made inhabitable by endless series of dikes, dams and bridges. At every bridge was a checkpoint, which meant travelling without travel papers was next to impossible.

The resistance fighters had organized a railroad strike during the bitterly cold winter of 1944-1945. They had no means to heat their home and survived by eating tulip bulbs and sugar beets. Albert's mother learned about a truck that was heading 150 miles north of The Hague, where they had relatives. Somehow, she bartered for seats in the back of an open truck, exposed to the brutal cold winter. They spent one day in The Hague to get paperwork processed for permission to travel out of the city. Traveling without paperwork was a death sentence. Miraculously, they were approved and were on the truck the next day.

They traveled only at night because anything moving during the day was targeted and destroyed by allied planes. The trip took three days, but they finally arrived in the countryside village. They ate a lot of rye, as that was what was available. It was wonderful. They could finally escape the masses of people, the noise and fear of rockets, and the desperate, constant feeling of hunger. However, within months, those would appear as luxuries to Albert--luxuries he would gladly embrace to be home again.

Exchanging One Occupation for Another

The occupation ended May 5, 1945. Albert and his family returned home on July 10, 1945. Healthcare, like many state-supported industries, had all but failed in the Netherlands as resources, travel, and support had dried up. To be sick at this time could turn deadly.

On November 14, 1945 Albert was diagnosed with Tuberculosis. Their doctor wanted Albert to be admitted to a hospital for immediate care, but with the hospital infrastructure decimated during the war, Albert's mother was afraid he would never come out alive. He was sent home and remanded to bed rest for a month.

Finally, on May 6, 1946, with Albert continuing to worsen, his mother agreed to send him to a sanatorium 100 miles from home. There were no facilities to care for Tuberculosis in the area, and specifically no pediatric facilities. What started as a plan for a month of treatment ultimately lasted more than two years in hospital and over three years of exclusive bed rest. For a young boy, this was a fate even worse than death.

Even though the war and occupation had ended, they had nothing. The family had relatives who had moved to California. They sent packages of food and supplies to Albert's family. In order to be admitted to the sanatorium for treatment, there was a list of things Albert had to bring.

One of the required items was five pairs of underwear. He didn't have them.

If it weren't for their family in California, Albert wouldn't have made it to the sanatorium for treatment.

This life without even the barest essentials exceeds the experiences of almost everyone in America today. No matter how desperate the conditions, finding and eating food of any quality, watching lice crawl in someone's hair, and ignoring the stench of an unbathed population can only be understood by a few.

Deep within the subconscious, Albert absorbed this agony as existence itself had stripped the smiles and the energy from a once vibrant population. Anger found its beginning within as oppression and ground up any hope for a return to their normal lives. Now Albert would be stripped from the only security he had left: his family.

The Sanatorium

Albert was placed in a ward with 10 boys, of which he was the youngest. For two years and five months, he endured the abuse of the older boys compounded by the confinement for his condition. Many of the younger boys were even placed in casts so they couldn't move.

He was nine years old with all of the energy and mischief of a boy, yet he was confined. He had to lay still, eat a lot, and get fresh air. That was the only treatment for Tuberculosis that they knew of at the time. If a patient couldn't lay still, they were bound to their bed. Depending on their condition, they graduated from 15 to 45 minutes a day out of bed, only allowed to lay on their sides between 1:00pm and 3:00pm.

A missionary came and blasted them with the belief that being sick was a consequence of sin. Albert interpreted his condition as being God's punishment for being a sinner. Since he had been sick so long, he reasoned that he must be going to Hell. He lived in fear long into his adulthood. As terrified as he was over this belief, he had no one to talk to about it.

Night after night he lay in quivering fear that he was worthless in the eyes of others, and even in the eyes of God.

His mother came every two weeks, when there was a bus she could take. She could only stay for a couple of hours each time she visited. Even with her visits, it was a horrible time for Albert that seemed to last forever, and he lived in a constant state of fear.

For a time, Albert's father was relocated with the patients of the mental hospital about six miles from the sanatorium. Once a week he visited Albert, walking the six miles with no complaints.

The worst part about Tuberculosis is that you don't feel sick, but you have to lay still. For a boy going through normal physical changes, it was miserable. Then he returned to a society that didn't even want him.

When Albert finally left the hospital in October of 1948, he was just as sick as when he went in. Now he stuttered and was so overweight that other kids made fun of him and called him "blubber." He didn't want to be seen by anyone. Resources were scarce, especially clothes, so nothing fit him.

Albert was determined to make up for lost time, but he couldn't help spending most of his time feeling angry. Why did God hate him? He didn't know, but the more he thought about the injustice of his life, the angrier he got.

From that point forward, a belief crept its way into Albert's thoughts. He was left behind and would never catch up. He believed he had missed so much education that he would always be pretending to know more than he actually knew. Even though it wasn't true, the lingering residue of those years left its mark. These beliefs further reinforced Albert's anger and cemented his belief that God was NOT on his side.

Intervention

After two years and five months in the sanatorium, Albert spent another six months recuperating at home until he was declared cured in April of 1949. During that time, an interesting thing happened. For some reason, one of his old school teachers, Mr. Veerbeek, took an unexplained interest in Albert's education. To hear Albert tell it, Mr. Veerbeek literally saved his life.

There wasn't much in the way of transportation available; it was not convenient. With Albert finally home, his teacher regularly visited him, even though it was a 25-minute bike ride to do so. He wasn't teaching anymore but had gone to school to become an attorney. He spent time tutoring Albert. By the time Albert made it home, he was thirteen with a third-grade education. Mr. Veerbeek gave Albert hope of a future.

After six months of tutoring, Albert had advanced three years in educational capability. He was ready to go back to school. If not for Mr. Veerbeek, Albert wouldn't have a prayer. Now, he felt up for the challenge.

During the most formative years of his life, Albert had seen only devastation, hunger, struggle, and pain. Now it was time to take control of his life with a vengeance. Fueled by a mix of anger and contempt, he found a fierce defiance that began to drive his independence.

It was a new day, and Albert was determined to pursue all that life had to offer.

Chapter 3 – Defiance

Albert was raised in a very conservative and strict Christian home. They prayed 11 times a day. They prayed first thing in the morning. Albert came home for lunch because the school was on the block, and they would pray. Every meal they prayed, ate, read the Bible, and then prayed again. At the Christian school Albert attended, they prayed at 9:00am, at 12:00pm, at 1:30pm and then at 3:30pm before they left for home. Every night they shared devotions in his home including prayer.

Bible history was part of the school curriculum as early as the first grade. Every Monday morning at school Albert had to recite a stanza from a memorized Psalm. All 150 psalms were converted into a Psalter so they could sing them. The 119th psalm had 81 stanzas. Every Monday, children had to learn and recite another psalm. Albert hated it.

His parents were sincere and strict. They were part of the Reformed (Calvinistic) tradition. The Calvinists teach "election," meaning that God elects who is going to Heaven or to Hell. Having heard this, Albert believed that no matter what he did, God had already made the decision. So, when he became sick, he believed God had it in for him.

The Alternative to God's Favor

When Albert was released from the hospital, the doctor told him he should never smoke due to the impact Tuberculosis had on his lungs. He was so defiant and angry that he started smoking only a few months after being declared well. He believed there was a God, but he believed God had destined him to Hell. The unfairness of it all burned inside him.

A battle began in Albert's mind that was often out of control. How could a loving God hate him so much? How could a loving God destine him to Hell? What had he done to deserve this?

A conflict was constantly brewing.

He knew there was a God and he desperately wanted to be loved by Him.

He wanted to prove that he was a good person and that God was wrong about him.

Moving On

Albert's family were common folk and never thought about going to university. Albert had been restrained his entire life, so he was now determined to make the most of life now that he was free of the hospital and the war. Determined to prove his worth (especially to God), he enrolled in a bookkeeping course in the evenings. As a result, he ended up with a job in social welfare. He genuinely liked helping people, and this was a chance to give care to others in a way that he wished it had been given to him.

He took a course in social work in the evenings to further expand his opportunities. And then an amazing thing happened: he was only 19, but when he met Theresa his life changed. The past began to fade and the future seemed bright with possibility. Finally, the sense of anger was met with the powerful acceptance of love. As their relationship grew, Albert knew he was ready to move from a devastating past into a new and powerful future with Theresa. He felt loved and needed like he never had before.

Albert and Theresa, 1956.

Post-War Challenges

Albert and Theresa were in love but getting married presented another problem for young couples in the post-war Netherlands. Rebuilding the country was in full swing but there was a housing crisis. The average couple was engaged for five years before marrying unless they moved in with their parents. Once again, Albert felt confined and restricted. He was not going to allow anyone else to dictate his future or hold him back.

Albert and Theresa talked about immigrating to Canada. Theresa had relatives there; it would be an opportunity to escape the economic difficulty at home. They dreamed of escaping the past, of living somewhere in peace for the first time. As children of the war and occupation, they both felt held back. Canada seemed like a perfect place to begin their new lives.

At the last minute, however, Albert was granted a Visa to the United States. He made the decision that they would move to the U.S. It would be a difficult transition because he could speak very little English. After much deliberation, he reasoned that the most important issue would be for him to have a good job in this new country. He quit his current job in the Netherlands and prepared for immigration by going to welding school for six months. Albert became proficient as an arc, electric, and gas welder. He hoped it would be enough.

Finally, Albert would have the chance to prove himself as a man, free from war, free from the confines of illness, free from the haunting taunts of cruel peers, and free from the constant reminder that he was not accepted or chosen by the God he had tried to serve.

Chapter 4 – The Land of Opportunity

In 1958, Albert and Theresa began the journey that would change the lives of thousands. Who could have pictured a couple of wide-eyed kids, barely out of their teens, standing on the dock that day, or known the destiny they were walking toward? Only God knew the impact this very helpless couple would have.

Albert would say this is the potential we all share, but this day in May of 1958 Albert and Theresa were boarding a ship that would bring them to the United States where their dream of a new life was waiting.

They were married in February and boarded the ship to New York in May. Landing in Hoboken, New Jersey, May 24, 1958, they stood on the docks with two suit cases and $88.00 in Albert's pocket. All their belongings were in their hands. At 21 years old they were starting over in a strange city and could barely communicate in this foreign language.

Being onboard the ship was an immediate improvement because food was readily available. When asked how he wanted his eggs prepared, he didn't know what they meant so he ordered two boiled, two scrambled and two over-easy. He laughs about it to this day.

They purchased train tickets to Momence, Illinois because Albert's sister had immigrated there.

After the train arrived in Chicago, they found that there was no train to Momence. On board the ship from the Netherlands, Albert had spent time helping another passenger during the ship-wide sickness. She was traveling alone and was also going to Chicago. She asked Albert and Theresa to stay with her on the train because she was desperately nervous about the trip. Albert didn't speak English well, but he wanted to be sure this new friend was taken care of.

When they reached Chicago, they waited with their traveling companion until a man came to pick her up at the train station. When he heard their story, he invited them to come to their home until they could figure out how to make it to Momence. Ultimately, the gentleman offered to drive them to Momence. It seemed like a miracle, in Albert's eyes.

There was no communication after they boarded the ship, so Albert's sister had no idea how or when they would arrive. She had rented an apartment down the street for Albert and Theresa. It was a tiny apartment costing $45.00 per month. His sister had worked hard to find some furniture, most of which was donated. All they had was the bare necessities, but they were thrilled to have a place to call home. The things Albert's sister had purchased had cost $125.00. Albert committed himself to paying her back.

Eisenhower was president and the economy was booming. Still, it took about three weeks for Albert to get a job. Meanwhile, he walked everywhere with no means of transportation.

Albert was still a very young man, but he had already weathered difficulty that was unimaginable. He tried to understand the perspectives of his new country where few had ever known hunger or watched the onslaught of soldiers. It was an exciting time and a confusing time. Albert felt free from the past and free to explore new possibilities, but also struggled with the limitations of culture and language.

Albert was determined to prove himself to Theresa, to his family, and to God. He was determined not to be held back by his sickness or the powerful emotions he'd struggled with when he was in his home country.

He was determined to show God that he had value and that he deserved more than he had experienced.

All he needed was a chance.

Chapter 5 – The TEST

With his training as a welder, Albert was able to get a job at Bennett Industries in Peotone, Illinois. His brother-in-law worked in the template room. Albert worked there until a big layoff in 1960, at which time he went to work on the table line at David Bradley (later becoming Roper Mfg.) in Kankakee.

Learning English in a factory environment might not have been the best way for Albert to adapt to this new culture. His language was crude and often vulgar, even if he didn't realize it. He was still smoking and began boozing it up with his friends after work instead of going home. His disdain for the past, and his anger for God and his past life, continued to fester as he hardened himself. He became more insensitive, especially to Theresa. He worked long hours and hung out with his work-mates, pushing aside her homesick loneliness. He remained confident both in God's existence and in his own predestined fate. Even while attending church and continuing his traditional heritage, Albert found himself frustrated and angry with God.

Albert – The Family Man

Diepeveen family in 1936.

Diepeveen family in the 1940s.

Diepeveen family in 2016.

Having parents with thick accents may have been the only dysfunction Ineke and Annette (Albert and Theresa's daughters) noticed in what could be described as a wonderful, boringly normal family life. Albert went to work, the girls went to school, and they were in church together every Sunday morning, Sunday night and Wednesday night. As Albert and Theresa had been raised, the Bible was read routinely, and prayer was offered both before and after every meal. The traditions were adhered to, even when it was obvious Albert really didn't want to.

As a welder, and then moving into piece work in assembly, Albert earned a very good wage at Roper. His $186.00 per week meant that he and Theresa could enjoy some of the things America had to offer. Albert never imagined himself as a businessman; he never dreamed what God had in mind for his future.

In every step, Albert saw himself as under-qualified, undeserving and lacking in almost every way. However, Albert soon learned that God's plan extended to much more than his eternal destiny. There is no way Albert could imagine what God would do with a simple Dutchman who eventually became willing to walk by faith.

The Visitor

Albert had the opportunity to meet an IBM executive from Holland who was a friend of a friend.

Computers were a mystical and almost impossible concept to grasp as Albert listened to this IBM executive talk about the future. Computers were starting to make an impact and it seemed that impact was going to spread farther in influence. Albert found himself extremely curious and through his questions was faced with an opportunity.

"There is a test."

Albert nearly flinched. School wasn't a fond memory and he felt much better with hands-on experience. Tests weren't easy or comfortable for him.

"The test is available through IBM and will indicate whether or not someone has the aptitude for computer programming. Based on our conversation, I think you should take that test. This is an emerging opportunity and I believe it could be a good fit for you, Albert. If you do well on that test, it's almost certain you will be able to get a job in this emerging field."

Albert laughed and dismissed it in his mind, although he was flattered by the compliment. Little did he know that this conversation wouldn't easily be forgotten. The possibility and the obvious potential were things he couldn't escape. There was no way to imagine what the future would hold for this struggling, stubborn Dutchman who was sure God had already given up on him.

If I'm going to make something of myself, it's up to me.

Albert turned out the light with determination that he would find a way to take this test. He would not be a factory worker for the rest of his life. He had to know if there was more out there for him.

Chapter 6 – A Giant Leap Forward

Making his way to the data processing department at Roper was like walking into the executive offices. As an assembly worker, Albert felt the pull of resistance with each step. He felt out of place. Dressed as a laborer, he couldn't imagine their opinion of him or how he could gain credibility in an area completely outside his skill set.

"I heard there's a test someone could take to determine whether they have aptitude in computer programming," stammered Albert. "I'd like to take that test."

There, he'd said it. Facing the head of data processing, he half expected the man to reach into his desk as if it were a standard application.

"We're not hiring," came the immediate reply. He looked over his desk at Albert, and after a long pause said, "And even if we were, we would be looking for people with experience. Do you have any experience?"

Albert's spine stiffened as he remembered what rejection felt like. He flashed to lingering abuse he faced as a child when nobody wanted him on their team. He felt heat on the back of his neck as he carefully replied, "I was encouraged to take the test by an IBM executive. He told me he believed I had the aptitude. Even if you're not hiring, I would like to take the test." Albert found resolve, as if the land of opportunity were somehow telling him otherwise. His accent was thick, but his eyes were piercing. He would not look away.

"I tell you what, Albert. I'll look into it, but this test is expensive. We don't just give it out. It would also waste hours of my day for me to administer it. Besides, I know the pay scale you're receiving now. Even if a job did open up in our department, it wouldn't even be close to what you're making. Check back with me in a couple of weeks."

Albert was certain the administrator expected him to forget all about it in the next couple of weeks. Feeling this challenge, however, triggered a defiant response. His imagination soared with images of working in a clean environment, being seen as a man of science instead of a laborer. It was no longer possible not to dream. His dreams told him that there was another door to walk through and he was determined to unlock it.

Undeterred

Albert became a familiar face in data processing as he made the trip, again and again. They needed to know he wasn't going away. He was serious. He didn't worry about the implications of the opportunity yet-- he only knew he wanted to have it. He had to know if he really did have what it took.

Finally, the decision was made, and he was informed that he would be granted a chance to take the test. Albert was both terrified and elated. Was it possible he had fantasized about this chance only to fail? He wondered if he had set himself up for embarrassment or if he was only kidding himself. He wished he'd already taken the test, so the torture of anticipation would be over.

When the day came, Albert didn't enter the room as a laborer. In his mind, he was already an executive. He had to pass this test. He would not go backward. He would not fall back to the limitations of the past.

He knew God was real, but would God dangle one more thing in front of him, only to taunt him?

Albert pushed the confusion of faith from his mind. It was long and laborious, then came the torturous wait for results. Albert soon learned that he had scored the second highest anyone had ever seen on the test. There were difficult decisions to be made if he were to pursue this course, but Albert knew one thing for certain: there was more going on than could be seen or imagined. For the first time in his life, Albert felt he had shown that God was wrong about him. And maybe God had agreed.

The Promotion

As often happens in life, advancement is hidden behind insecurity and risk. Now that Albert was 'on the list' with the data processing department, he knew there would be a big decision to be made once they were ready to hire. Undoubtedly with his test score, the opportunity would be offered to him.

Albert and Theresa could finally afford furniture that wasn't borrowed. They felt some benefit from Albert's hard work and his $186.00 per week paycheck. However, Albert knew that if he took a job in data processing, his pay would be cut, literally, in half. At 30 years old, with two children and a mortgage, reality loomed heavily.

Albert and Theresa crafted a budget that could accommodate the reduction in pay. After the bare essentials, only $17.00 per week remained for food and clothing. There would be nothing frivolous, likely for years. They had both lived in post-war poverty and had escaped it. Now he would be asking his young wife to make this sacrifice that would place them back into financial duress.

Albert struggled with his own motivation. Was it selfish? Did he have a future in computer programming or was he losing his seniority for nothing?

He couldn't make such a decision. He had placed himself first too many times already. He'd spent time and money to satisfy his own wants and now he was asking Theresa to suffer further while he pursued his dreams. Love goes farther than Albert knew it could. Even then, God's love was unfolding; that day it was through the open thoughts and heart of Theresa.

"You need to find a way to do this, Albert," came Theresa's shocking words. "I believe you need to do this. God will take care of us."

If you've ever wondered how love expresses itself or how its roots could go deep enough to withstand a lifetime, Albert was lucky enough to learn of this. Not only was he loved by Theresa, his often taken-for-granted wife, she believed in him and had been willing to place him ahead of everything else.

Albert was ready when the day finally came. $92.00 a week working second shift from 4:00pm to 12:00am. He learned so much. He never stopped reaching beyond what was expected and took the challenges nobody else wanted. He continually took IBM courses that were available on his own time. He took tests every week to see where he stood.

The lack of money and added stress were met with enthusiastic creativity by Theresa. It never occurred to the girls how poor they really were because of Theresa's outspoken support and love for her husband. She had learned to survive and thrive through her closely-knit family. Her perspective and joy for life energized the family, and propelled Albert as he clung to her belief, at times even more than his own. Fierce and loving teamwork bridged the gap when others might have failed.

It simply never occurred to Theresa that any other path would substitute for the hard-fought dream her husband diligently pursued. Together they would thrive, regardless the obstacles.

Finally, after two years in operations at that same $92.00 per week, Albert was a standout in his department. When opportunity came, Albert was ready. A position opened up for a programmer and Albert got the job. Others with more seniority in the data processing department wanted the position, but everyone knew that Albert had earned it. Everyone knew that he would be successful.

Looking back, some might say it's a fairytale with thread woven through Albert's life into a fabric that would comfort generations to come.

At the time it seemed like a financial decision, but indeed it was a breakthrough from the limits of the past to a future being orchestrated by a loving God.

Chapter 7 – The Reluctant Entrepreneur

After two years as a programmer at Roper Corporation, opportunities started coming from everywhere. Albert had distinguished himself in this emerging field and soon began experiencing endless possibilities.

Albert accepted a position as a programmer with Jones and McKnight, a steel company. Soon he was the head of the programming department. Eventually, he launched a service business within Jones and McKnight. It was Albert's proposal to capitalize on the powerful computer system the company had purchased. It had a huge amount of excess capacity and Albert saw the potential to expand his reach.

Albert developed the new division, populating it with customers who needed capacity and couldn't justify their own large computer infrastructure investment. Albert programmed for these customers and leased time on the mainframe for their business. He didn't realize he was preparing himself to be a businessman, and that God was building his business right before his eyes.

Although Albert's service division of Jones and McKnight was profitable, the steel business itself went into bankruptcy in the 1970s. Their bankruptcy created a separation between Albert's division and the main company. Albert was literally forced into business for himself because Jones and McKnight needed his services as an independent contractor and he didn't want to let down the customers he'd developed and programmed for.

Albert leased time at night on the mainframe at Kankakee Community College when the computer was not in use. He moved all of the service customers to that system. Suddenly, he was faced with the reality of being in business for himself. Like many in business, Albert quickly became a workaholic. He worked nights when the computer was available, and worked days developing customers and new business.

In 1973, Albert formed a company called Datafax. Soon he was able to purchase the computer from the steel company due to their bankruptcy, and he moved all of his customers to it. Business grew, and Albert began to prosper. Somehow all of this had grown from the seed of that scary test and Theresa's belief some six years before. God was at work in Albert's life. The momentum brought its own potential for good and for evil. Soon, Albert would face the realities that come for the one who believes in God but runs a business in the 'real world.'

Chapter 8 – Unexpected Awakening

By age 40, Albert had found a rhythm for business and developed a reputation for getting things done. He was proud of his reputation. If he said he was going to do something, he did it. The computer and data processing businesses were growing and so was Albert's success.

Also at age 40, as Albert began a new decade of life, he didn't realize that another great change would present itself. Like each of the decades before, the war, the hospital, leaving his homeland, and struggling to begin a new career, this decade seemed destined to begin with sacrifice. With lack of understanding. Even with a continuing hostility toward God.

Albert grew up in the church and he always believed in God, but it was a tenuous relationship. Albert felt it was a one-way street. He tried to worship but remained haunted by the belief that God had no place for him. He was certain through the circumstances of his boyhood that he was not part of God's elect. Even though it was buried deep inside, Albert's view of God in his life was void. He felt destined to go it alone.

Having experienced the trauma of sickness and confinement for years in a hospital, Albert found himself angry with God when he learned that the wife of his lifelong friend had been diagnosed with fast-acting MS. Albert flew to Canada, where they lived, to offer physical and financial support.

Andy and Albert's friendship began before they were even born. Their mothers were girlfriends and pregnant at the same time. They grew up together. When Albert returned from the hospital as a boy, Andy defended him against bullies. Andy was his protector. Albert could still remember a time when Andy threw rocks at kids who were making fun of him.

When Albert was held back in school because he was so far behind, Andy purposefully let his schoolwork slide so he could be in the same class as Albert. They were inseparable, a bond strong enough to last a lifetime.

When Andy immigrated to Canada, their friendship remained as strong as ever. When Albert received the news that Andy's wife, Diana, was stricken with MS, he was angry, particularly with God. It brought back deep and familiar agony from Albert's past illness and his blame toward God. It was deeper than Albert realized.

When Albert arrived in Montreal, he didn't find Diana and Andy feeling sorry for themselves. Instead of despair over her situation, Diana beamed with confidence and joy. Albert was sure it was a momentary thing. He was sure she hadn't yet accepted her situation, especially when she told him that she was thankful to God for everything that was happening to her.

His own experiences in tow, Albert told Diana that she was only talking that way because she wanted God to heal her. Albert poured out his heart with the failure of his own pleas and promises to God as a boy.

"It doesn't work," he argued. "I made all kinds of promises to God and He didn't do a thing!"

A smiling Diana calmly replied, "Yes, Albert, but you didn't do what I did. You didn't ask Jesus into your heart." Albert had never heard of this before.

He was sure her good attitude wouldn't last, but over time he saw her peace continue and even expand to everyone around her. Secretly, Albert was jealous because he had never found peace; not in the hospital and not in business. Even though she was never to walk again, Diana's life had changed, and it became a watermark in his life. If God could really do this, maybe there was something to this 'born again' idea.

Being Thankful

Meanwhile, a new pastor came to Albert's church. A former school teacher, he had come to know Christ later in life through his adopted daughter. Albert saw the same peace in him that he had seen in Diana.

Albert couldn't imagine why this man, who talked about God's grace, would come to preach to a bunch of legalistic Dutchmen. Soon they became friends, even though Albert was far from buying into his message.

Albert loved time in church because it gave him quiet to do his own problem solving. Once, in the middle of a sermon, Albert stood and blurted, "I got it," because he had realized the solution to a programming problem. A little embarrassed, he tried to pretend he was paying attention for the rest of the service.

One day his pastor, Vern Smith, told him that he needed to accept Christ. Albert replied with such intensity and conviction that it shocked his new friend.

Soon afterward, Vern was preaching from 1 Thessalonians 5:18. "Give thanks in all circumstances." In that preaching he said that if someone loves you they will never let anything happen to you that is not good for you. Albert thought that made sense. Vern used the example of Corrie Ten Boom. She was a Dutch lady who was with her sister in a concentration camp during the war. They somehow smuggled in a Bible. They read and prayed constantly but Corrie was still filled with anger toward her captors. Meanwhile, her sister prayed and thanked God for the fleas that were tormenting them because they kept the guards from coming around. Her sister never made it out of the concentration camp, but her prayer of thanks left a mark on Corrie. It changed Corrie into a powerful Christian who was able to ultimately embrace her Nazi captors and pray for them, even love them long after the war.

This story awakened Albert. He thought about his daughter who was going to the University of Illinois. When she was home, Albert insisted she be home by 11:00pm. She thought Albert hated her, but he did it because he loved her. Suddenly it hit him.

"Maybe God does love me." He couldn't imagine it, but it felt strangely right. His relationship all these years was based on the feeling that God did not love him. When Vern said to him, as a friend, that God loved him, the light went on. Albert was not Bible ignorant but realized he had based his beliefs on feelings about himself. Somehow, in that moment, he felt God's love for him.

This changed Albert's life. Vern asked Albert to start thanking God, *no matter what*. Albert felt excited about the prospect. For so long his only prayers had been automatic, and now he would be praying from his heart.

Bible study in a parliament building in Budapest, Hungary.

The next day, he started praying. *Thank you, Lord, for this day.* It felt weird. He went through the mail later that day and saw a bill from his attorney. It was higher than he expected, but he was prompted to say, "Thank you, God." The words just came out and he paused to laugh at himself. He felt peace. He continued to be thankful in all things, remembering that God loved him and wouldn't let anything happen to him that wasn't good for him.

Even with this new awareness, Albert struggled with the effort to consciously thank God. Still, he had promised to do so, and he was a man of his word. After about two weeks of struggle he impulsively did something that he thought was completely sissy-like. He got on his knees and told God that he needed him to come into his life. He didn't feel different, but he believed the Bible was true and that God had been knocking on his heart's door for 40 years. If he would come now, Albert would welcome him in. In that moment, he felt God come in.

Since that vivid moment, Albert began to live with the awareness of God's presence, His love and His blessings. He has never been the same. For the first time, he actually believed he was going to heaven.

For the first time, he felt the whole load of fear and guilt fall off.

Albert found peace.

Chapter 9 – The Coalition

What had begun as an experiment had given Albert a new definition for success. The decision to be thankful in all circumstances transformed Albert. Taking action every day on that decision opened his eyes.

"God will not allow anything to happen in my life that is not for my good. I may not understand it, but when I stand on that truth from God's words, I know I am free from everything that is trying to destroy me." Albert claimed this truth in every conversation, every affirmation, and with every struggle he encountered. Somehow, it became unimaginable for him to look at any circumstance without believing it was within God's capacity to bring good into his life.

When that kind of change happens, the ripple effect bounces off of every obstacle. Albert was to find that not everyone could appreciate what he had come to know, especially in the church.

In a men's prayer group, Albert requested prayer for a difficult situation he was facing in his business. Later, he learned that one of the men in the group had expressed disbelief that Albert had asked for prayer when God had already blessed him with a business, unlike most in the group. Albert realized that there was a distinct difference between perspectives represented there, and he wondered how many others felt the same. He also wondered how many people in business, who were Christians, felt unable to share their struggles and ask for prayer when others could not relate.

Albert made the decision that he would seek out other Christian business leaders where he could discuss the unique challenges of business and seek counsel. Soon, he had an idea. It was risky. It made him feel uneasy and vulnerable, but he and a likeminded group of his friends began making a list of area business people they thought might be interested in just such a coalition.

Staring at this list of more than 100 names, Albert prepared a letter. His heart pounded as he imagined it being read by businessmen, wondering if it would be heard or accepted by them. He stared at the completed draft for two weeks before finally placing the stack of envelopes into the mail. A response was required, but would they respond? Would they take him seriously? Would they find it valuable enough to join?

Albert imagined a handful of men might answer with positive responses. Imagine his shock when more than 80 responses poured in. The possibility could now be a reality. Albert was elated. It was another step toward the exponential impact God had in mind for this stubborn Dutchman.

Albert had no idea where to begin, but as per usual, he was thankful to God for whatever He was doing.

Listening to Moody Radio, Albert began to hear about CBMC and what they called "marketplace ministries." It was critical for businessmen to bond together for the application of faith and to share in their needs and prayers. This seemed like a perfect chance to partner with an organization that already had a strategy. Albert quickly learned more about CBMC and how they could launch a chapter in Kankakee.

The Kankakee chapter was organized with more than 80 members in business. Albert led the group, and so began a process that he would participate in locally, nationally and internationally. From this meager beginning came relationships and powerful opportunities for Christian businessmen to bond for the Glory of God.

Albert's passion for sharing the power of God's principles in business with other business leaders soon set him apart as a leader. Even after more than four decades in organizational leadership, seminars and constant mentoring of other business leaders, Albert still sees himself as unqualified. He can't imagine how he could be used in these ways or why he would be given so much honor.

The true measure, in Albert's words, is what God can do through His people.

"If you want to see what God can do, start by being thankful to Him in all circumstances.

When you do that, you can't help but see God at work in everything. Nothing else can make you happy. Nothing else is worth holding on to. It's an adventure with more rewards than money could ever buy. It's the only way you can live with *no regrets*."

Chapter 10 – The Covenant

It was 1980, some four years after Albert asked God to come into his life. Albert had been working actively in CBMC for some time. He kept the formula simple: thank God in all things and learn what God says about business. He supported others and found a deep sense of contentment in his young relationship with God.

Albert's first international CBMC function
in the Netherlands, October 1981.

In October of 1980, Albert and Theresa attended the Praise Gathering in Indianapolis with two close friends. Tony Compolo, Debbie Boone, Larry Burkette and many others spoke at the event. Larry Burkette even held a workshop on the biblical principles of business.

In the car on the way home, the couples talked about the event. Albert's friend had attended Larry Burkett's seminar. As they discussed the workshop in detail, Albert learned that Larry believed, as Christians, everyone should be out of debt so as to be good stewards of God's resources. If you borrow it should be with a specific means of repayment because of what the Bible says about being debtors. Apparently, Larry felt that being in debt was like a Christian being in bondage.

After a great deal of discussion on the topic, Albert found himself saying to Theresa, "I don't know why I am saying this but we're going to get out of debt."

Theresa's immediate response was, "I wonder what God has in mind for us?"

Albert and Theresa had no idea what would be required to get out of debt, but they prayed that God would make it possible. It seemed selfish when God had provided so much, but Albert knew that if God would tell him to do it, then God would make a way for it to happen.

Albert and Theresa, present day.

A month later, Albert started hemorrhaging and coughing up blood. In the hospital they did a bronchoscopy and were certain he had cancer in the left lung. They stopped the bleeding but sent him to Cleveland Clinic to have it further looked into. It was just before Christmas when he arrived. They ran tests and did a biopsy to diagnose his condition. After giving him a favorable initial response, they sent him home to enjoy the holidays.

Christmas was wonderful. Albert enjoyed family and expressed his thankfulness to God for the favorable responses from his doctors. However, the doctor called after Christmas and told him that he did, after all, have cancer. They believed it was an aggressive cancer that must be addressed now. They wanted him to return as soon as possible.

Theresa was also struggling with some physical difficulties at the time. The first trip to Cleveland Clinic pushed her to her physical limit. It was so taxing on her that Albert didn't want to tell her about the call he'd received.

As Albert was deeply in prayer, he remembered once again that God had told him to be thankful in all circumstances. He thanked God right then for these difficult situations. In the fervor of this belief he could not keep the information from Theresa. He had to share.

God was at work and Albert had chosen to give thanks, even in these unexplainable and awful circumstances. He could not choose the circumstances, but he could choose his response.

After New Year's Eve they traveled to Cleveland Clinic. Hundreds, maybe even thousands, were praying relentlessly, petitioning God for healing on Albert's behalf. Albert couldn't pray for himself because he knew that whatever God was doing, it was for his good. Still, the power of so many praying for him was both humbling and comforting.

Surgeons removed the lower lobe of Albert's left lung. It was a horribly painful surgery. They had to spread apart his ribs to get to his lungs, so the recovery was very difficult. Days later, Albert anxiously awaited his prognosis.

"Albert," the doctor began, "There is good news and there is bad news. The good news is that there is no cancer. The bad news is that you never had cancer in the first place."

Albert was elated. God had performed a miracle. The doctors and the hospital, however, had a much different approach. They were consumed with concern for the liability issues. Apparently, the hospital felt the pathologist had made a mistake with the biopsy. They were posturing to deal with the blame. Albert announced that he held no one responsible and they did not need to worry about him suing anyone. Albert, if you can imagine, was simply *thankful.*

In All Things: God

While Albert and the hundreds who were praying for him rejoiced, the hospital was still grappling with how this could happen. They weren't satisfied with Albert's assessment of the situation. They wanted to know how they could make this right. From a liability perspective, that meant a monetary payment. The hospital administration and lawyers wanted to know what they could do to gain a release from liability.

Amazingly, Albert asked if they would be willing not to charge him for his medical treatment. They insisted there must be more than that. Albert presented a small bill for his expenses for the trip and asked if they thought it was reasonable. Nobody could believe it.

Albert began receiving calls and mail from attorneys who wanted to represent him in his case. "We can get you $500,000 in these types of situations," he was told by a legal representative. Still, Albert remained firm. He was just thankful to be alive and healthy.

The hospital was so paranoid about their liability, they still sent him a check. Albert didn't like it and was determined to give the money away. Theresa, however, felt that God was involved. She reminded Albert that they had been praying for a way to get out of debt and they should honor God by taking the money. With the check, a tax refund and cashing in a life insurance policy, they were able to get completely out of debt in March of 1981, just six months after Albert had proclaimed he believed God wanted them to get out of debt.

"God won't give you a principle you can't implement."

Albert remains firm to this day that if we are willing to follow God's plan, we can count on results. Is it possible that God not only answered the prayer for Albert's healing, but used it to fulfill Albert's prayer to be out of debt?

"I don't have to understand," Albert affirms. "I just have to trust Him. He said we could test Him with our finances. That's the only place He says to test Him."

From a business perspective, it didn't make sense for Albert to pay off his loan at 5.25% on his home. His savings was earning 12% at the time. However, God had told him to get out of debt. As it turns out, the bank was so glad to see him coming they offered him a discount to pay off the loan. God worked out every step of the process.

"We forget so easily all that God has done for us," says Albert. "When I spend time in gratitude, it helps me never to forget. It gives me strength to look past today's problems and thank God for them too. If I try to solve problems on my own, I just get in the way of what God is planning."

Chapter 11 – Never a Hero

Why is it that our tendency is to put people on pedestals and call them out as heroes? Why do we need them? Albert struggled with his own healing and his own story of blessing because he knew he was never a hero. When Albert had cancer, the whole world had people praying for him, but he couldn't pray for himself. Why would God heal him over others? Albert believed passionately that his only purpose was to stay inside God's will and to be thankful in all circumstances.

It was so much easier to promote others than to promote himself. Albert felt he had no unique qualities, no high degree of intelligence, and no real gifts. He knew only a few simple things and his entire life was built on repeating those truths.

1. I will thank God for everything, no matter what.

2. I know that God will never do anything that is bad for me, even if I don't understand it.

3. I know that God will never give me a principle in His Word that cannot be implemented.

Now Albert would step into some new concepts which would test his belief and his rationale as a businessman. These challenges would cause him to add one more very big statement to his credo. Albert was soon to speak a statement which would forever alter his business life, his influence, and even put him at odds with others who would become polarized by his radical stance.

4. I will never again borrow money for any purpose. I will be a lender, but I will never again become a borrower.

Regardless of the arguments and the power of logic concerning business borrowing, Albert never tried to place his personal conviction on anyone else. He just knew that he would never borrow again. Why? The Word of God placed such clarity between the borrower and the lender. There was never anything good said about being a debtor. In order to identify himself further with God's Word and God's success principles, Albert had to think in terms of this absolute. God had made a way for him to get out of debt and he was never going to go backwards with God.

Little did Albert know the impact of this stance or the path that would result.

Maximum Income Philosophy

As Albert's leadership and involvement in CBMC grew, so did his relationship with great men like Larry Burkett. Albert and Larry discussed financial business philosophies. They discussed the concept of OPM: Other People's Money. As a business growth philosophy, OPM had become the weapon of choice for business to grow through leverage.

As they discussed the dangers and pitfalls of this business model, Larry asked Albert a curious question. "Have you ever considered a Maximum Income Philosophy?"

Albert had never even heard of such a concept, but it intrigued him. The concept implied that a disciplined Christian would determine how much money was 'enough' and give everything else away. It was an expression of the ultimate trust that God would provide, therefore we do not need to have a "Plan B."

Albert found it to be a liberating concept. As his business grew, he found himself giving much of his income to various charities but never quite found a way to define it. Albert discussed the idea with Theresa and they decided to limit their income and give the rest to others. So, he set his maximum income at a modest level, even though at that time he was making much more.

A new paradigm had been added to Albert's beliefs as his study of Christian leadership principles continued. It freed him from the impulses to buy a bigger home or a nicer car. It freed him to look for ways to use his income to expand the kingdom of God through investing in God's people, especially those in desperate need.

International Ministry

Albert's involvement in CBMC evolved with his leadership of the international board in the late 80s. Eastern Europe opened up and Albert traveled there many times to minister, specifically to those who had been under communist influence. Business owners in eastern Europe now had opportunity but had no idea how to run a business, especially as a Christian. Albert found it troubling that so many in the world would give their lives for Jesus but didn't know anything about biblical business principles.

Talking biblical principles in Eastern Europe with Brother Andrew, 1994.

Albert had attended a seminar led by Larry Burkett entitled "Business by the Book." After the seminar, he realized how important it was to help people understand biblical business principles. He learned that it was the second most talked about subject in the Bible, second only to love. As successful as many Christian business owners were, most didn't know anything about God's perfect plans for business. Albert knew this was a mission he had to take on.

You go to school so you can earn money. You work for money and after you are done working you think about how you are going to spend the money. Money is the most important topic that is consistent with everyone on earth. God has principles for it and Albert wanted to share them. He got the materials from Larry, Howard Dayton and others, then simplistically tried to share it in Eastern Europe. There were many who wanted to be in business but had no clue how to do it.

Albert created his own way of teaching those principles. Ultimately, he got involved with Larry Burkett and learned to teach the "Business by the Book" seminar. With Don Delosier as a mentor, Albert lead the seminar around the world. He had the opportunity to share God's plan for business with thousands of leaders.

The process initiated by CBMC was to introduce people to Jesus and then to disciple them. Once people saw biblical business principles in action, they were already being discipled. It was always more about discipleship than anything, and Albert felt deeply aligned with that mission.

Albert became determined to awaken the Christian business community to the powerful principles of God. He imagined every day that business leaders were being deceived and could come to a perspective of freedom through the blessings inherent in God's existing business plan. He persisted sacrificially in this message, dreaming of a day when young business owners would be mentored in a path of discipline to God's principles rather than today's culture of greed.

Albert was always quick to share his own experiences and stories, but also added, "Just because God deals with me specifically about not borrowing at all and declaring a maximum income philosophy, doesn't mean that's what God is telling you to do. Finance is the one area God says clearly that we should test him. I can't imagine how much interest I would have paid if I hadn't listened and obeyed God."

Faith is not a feeling. You must make decisions about what you are going to do.

Whatever you place your faith in will be the basis for your decisions, whether you feel it or not.

There is a difference between saying you are going to do something and when you *tell God* you are going to do, or not do, something. When Albert told God that he was not going to borrow money ever again, it was more powerful than just saying it to himself.

"I told God I wasn't going to do it and I'm not going to go back on my word. It's not my problem anymore. It's His. He said I could test Him and He has always been faithful."

Chapter 12 – My Portion

Albert lived in a complicated world with a deep desire to keep his life simple. Every day he asked God, "What *is* my portion?" He believed so vividly that God was walking with him and taking care of him that he set a limit on his lifestyle and on his income. Many years, he gave away more than he kept. He saw God's blessings as a wonderful chance to invest in what God was doing by giving them away.

If he hadn't done that, he would have bought bigger homes, bigger cars, *bigger.* Instead, he learned how to be strategic about giving it away. It became fun, a challenge, an excitement to see what God would bring his way and how he could make an impact on the lives of others. As his thankfulness increased, he saw things change.

"What is our greatest problem really?" Albert asks. "It's this idea that we need to know what to *do.* God doesn't send you a letter to tell you. He doesn't have an app. We just do what we believe is right and we listen all the time for God to tell us to stop! To close the door! We count on God to lead."

As Albert came into this state of living he wanted to share it with other people, but initially he was afraid to do it. Still, he knew he had to share it. He took hold of Jesus' words in John 14 where he said, "I brought you glory on the earth from doing the things you gave me to do." What did Jesus do on earth? He told people about the Father; about His nature and His Kingdom. That was all. Albert was sure that this was his call as well; to tell people what God's Kingdom was like, right here on the earth. Right here in business.

"God is in control of everything and He will never give you a principle you cannot implement." Albert began saying this to himself daily, and soon it was the mantra he shared openly. If you've ever had a conversation with Albert, you've heard him say it. "God says we can test him in this." Albert did test God and it became a lifestyle he couldn't resist.

He became like a child again as he realized that all he had to do in life was to glorify God. It became so real to him that it was completely liberating. He discovered the difference between knowing about God and knowing God. He felt God's ownership in his life and that meant God owned his business as well. He saw God as the owner and he was running the business for God. No matter what we build in this life, we can't take any of it with us. "Even your shoelaces are His," Albert quipped.

Building the Business

Borrowing money was not an option from Albert's perspective, but he needed to purchase a computer for the business. This was long before any concept of personal computers. Computers were expensive and exclusive. Albert prayed about how to accomplish this and struck on the idea of approaching his customers to partner with him in the purchase. He reasoned that he could afford to pay interest on their equity investment at a good rate and they would be equity owners rather than lenders. He formed 'computer partners' and it became another perfect example of God's principles at work.

Rather than being passive investors in his company, Albert's customers/partners soon became some of his greatest salesmen. They told everyone they knew about Albert's services. The business grew beyond Albert's wildest dreams as a result.

"This idea of never borrowing money," Albert cautioned, "isn't for everyone. I know there is proper use of borrowing. I believe God was clear with me about it and I promised I wouldn't do it, so I haven't. There isn't anything good said about being a debtor in God's Word. I simply believe that God is my provider.

I don't see anywhere in His Word that the solution to a problem is to go into debt. He says that He is the solution.

I know I'm extreme, but this is my choice. I want to depend completely on God. I can't tell anyone else what they should do."

Building the Business, Part II

Through a migration of business platforms, Albert soon became highly valued by Honeywell's computer division. He found himself one day on a jet flying to Honeywell for training at their expense. Sitting with Albert was another business owner. As they talked, Albert found they had similar business, both in size and duration. His counterpart had borrowed and invested $1,000,000 in the startup of his business. Albert had accomplished the same results for around $5,000 invested. Albert wondered what all would be possible to accomplish for God's glory with the interest he was not paying on $1,000,000 of debt.

It's Only a Signature

As technology progressed, the time came that Albert knew his business needed an updated computer with more power and memory. He had over 20 employees. Business was exciting and profitable. Albert continued giving away the excess above his maximum income and found himself responsible for placing God's money where it could be the most effective.

Two of Albert's customers/equity partners had sold their business and offered to help him purchase a new computer in a manner similar to the existing arrangement with Computer Partners. As part of selling the old computer and purchasing a new one, all they wanted Albert to do was cosign the note. It was totally in Albert's favor to do so.

Albert was excited about the growth opportunity, but the night before he was to meet his partners at the bank, he was unable to sleep. He hadn't intended to ignore his commitment not to borrow, but he had rationalized that he was not the borrower. He agonized all night over the issue and once morning came he knew he had to have a very uncomfortable face-to-face with his partners.

"I'm not going to cosign." Albert put the facts on the table.

The reply from his partners was perverse and angry, as Albert had expected. "Are you really willing to put those 20 people out of a job because of your silly principles?"

"All I know is that I can't cosign. I told God I wasn't going to do it and I'm not going to go back on my word." (Proverbs 17:18)

The deal was already in place and the paperwork prepared. Albert was drawing a line in the sand. He calmly smiled as he placed the entire future of his business in God's hands, right in the middle of the conflict.

God had given him the business. God had provided in the past. He knew that no matter what, God had a plan and he was willing to let God have leadership in every financial matter.

Within a matter of days, something interesting happened. Albert received a call from his potential equity partner. "Albert did you a huge favor," his accountant told the partner as he evaluated the impact of the transaction. "If you had continued as planned, you would have structured this incorrectly." With some key changes, his partner would receive much more favorable tax advantages and it was all due to Albert's unwillingness to cosign the deal.

The computer was purchased without Albert as a cosigner and once again the outcome was better than anyone could have planned. God had blessed Albert, and everyone associated with him, because Albert was brave enough to put God first.

"I told God I wasn't going to borrow money ever again and I wasn't going to go back on my word."

It may have seemed like a foolish financial decision to most, but for Albert it was a matter of trust. He trusted God and he was willing to test God and keep his hands off.

It was another step in the journey which pioneered for many a divine belief. Albert dared to live on a principle in God's Word, no matter what the perceived consequences were.

Chapter 13 – The Divine Experiment

Early in Albert's experiment with God's provision, he made a decision. II Corinthians 9:6 reverberated through Albert's thoughts as he imagined the economics of God's Kingdom. "Remember this: whoever sows sparingly will also reap sparingly, and whoever sows generously will also reap generously." He knew in Malachi 3:10 God himself said, "Test me in this and see if I will not throw open the floodgates of Heaven and pour out so much blessing that there will not be room enough to store it."

Albert knew that the consuming desire to see God's presence manifest in his life meant that he would have to test it. He also knew it might not always seem like the logical thing to do.

The desire to experience everything God had in store meant that he would have to believe what God said.

Truly believing meant taking action based on that belief. It was exciting and scary all at the same time.

Much like Albert's initial choice to "be thankful in all circumstances," he felt compelled to begin a new experiment. Before he could back out of the inspiration to do so, he told his secretary to write a check for $1,000 every Friday. He would give it away. She thought he was nuts. It was early in his business and the previous year they had barely broken even. Soon after they started the process, she informed Albert they didn't have the money to write the check, but he told her to write it anyway.

After nine weeks, the checks hadn't bounced but Albert started to get scared. *Who am I to test God? What are you doing, Albert? How can it be that we didn't make any money last year and I am giving this money away? What if I--* So, he quit doing it.

At the end of the quarter, his bookkeeper had to go to Hilton Head to work on something for another company and he wanted to take Albert's books so he could work on them. He called the next day and asked Albert if he was nuts. He had already given away $9,000.

Albert apologized to his bookkeeper and then explained why he'd done it. As it turned out, Albert had not only given away $9,000 but he'd profited $9,000 in that very time frame. Albert realized that when he had trusted God, God had poured out blessings.

This experience became a turning point in Albert's choice to trust God "in all things."

A Loving Father

Spending time with God became the strength for business that Albert clung to. His ownership of trust began in his vision of God as a loving father. He reasoned that a loving father would never let something bad happen to him.

Soon another question emerged: "How can we give something to God that already belongs to Him?" God already owned everything, including Albert's business. He was simply the manager.

The premise of trusting God became the paradigm for Albert's decision making. Trusting God in his finances really wasn't about money, it was about looking to God as the one who provides for our needs.

If we can't trust him with our needs, then we don't trust him at all.

Albert had also seen people die of hunger while trusting God. It was a hard truth to understand but he still chose to believe it.

Perhaps Albert's desires changed or perhaps it was the overwhelming satisfaction he felt when he was actively involved in trusting God beyond his own ability to understand. Whatever the case, Albert grew personally, and his business grew as he tested and trusted God. "That is the only way to learn," said

Albert. "If you never really trust, you can never learn or experience the result of that trust."

Albert couldn't wait to continue the process of giving away $1,000 a week. At one point, Albert was giving away $25,000 a month, even though it wasn't always easy.

Albert believed in the open-hand economics of God's Kingdom. He first learned this from a close friend and leader, Ron Blue. Whatever God placed in his hand, he would use for God's Kingdom. The joy of being part of this process became the joy of living. Albert saw many other businessmen bound by debt while using their profits to pursue material gratification. Albert never criticized them, but he continued to look for ways to share this powerful truth.

Albert never owned a new car or moved into a big home. He preferred to exchange it all for a relationship of power, pleasure and peace in a humble relationship with God. All the while, his business prospered.

Chapter 14 – Don't Be Confused

The more Albert shared his "Business by the Book" philosophy, the more confused people he heard from. They believed what Albert was teaching meant they would have to ignore good business principles. They felt he was telling them to throw conventional planning and execution to the wind.

Albert didn't understand why they would believe he was advocating such a procedure but soon realized that often business owners see these as the two extremes. They believed he was telling them not to listen to the advice of others. It was an issue that had to be addressed.

Advance planning is absolutely a responsibility for the Christian business leader. There must also be a process, a specific set of standards, that are the foundation for those plans and advice. Albert listened to his bookkeeper, for example, in those early days of extreme giving, but ultimately, he compared what he knew with God's promises. What had developed as a logical process for Albert had to become a practical teaching he could share.

Albert arrived at these simple distinctions:

1. The Word of God says you need counsel. Get counsel but seek your counsel among those

who are demonstrating their own dependence on God.

2. Ask yourself, "Is God going to get the Glory for this?" Plan your lifestyle, don't just plan your business. Never forget that your plans represent how you define your actual trust in God more than anything else.

3. Ask yourself, "Are my plans breaking any biblical principles?"

4. Realize that eventually your plans need to be blessed by the Holy Spirit. If your plans fit all of the other criteria, proceed with them and pray constantly that God will change your direction if it's not His plan.

"If you keep these things in mind and are using them as the foundation for your planning, you're building on a solid foundation," Albert shared. "The Holy Spirit lives within us and the Bible says it's the same Spirit that raised Christ from the dead. When we ask for wisdom, we will receive it. *If you are on the wrong track but you really want God's will, you will know it.*"

Do Not Store Up Treasures on Earth

Albert grappled with another conflicting issue related to God's blessings in his business. Albert sought clarity in an area most would never consider. He knew it needed a distinction. The Bible speaks about being a lender and not a borrower, but what did it mean to be a lender? A lender implied that we would have excess and in order to pile up excess one would have to store things up. Yet, the Bible clearly said we should not store up treasures on earth. This troubled Albert.

Was it a matter of faith, or was it a difference in perspective?

Before Albert had even become a Christian, his pastor asked him to allow his name to be run on the ballot to become a deacon in their church. He didn't want to do it. He felt hypocritical. He knew he was not living right with God. Eventually he allowed his name to be run. Then he was scared he might actually be elected, so he didn't go to church for six weeks. They elected him anyway.

He went to the first meeting and he wasn't happy to be there. Why? He felt uncomfortable challenging the thinking of the church leaders, but he had disagreements in how they were functioning. Even though he was not a Christian at the time, he knew what God's Word said and had strong opinions about it.

"You have a loan on the church and every month you have a building collection. You raise money but pay only the necessary payment. Then you use the rest to build up reserves of cash. Meanwhile, you have money and there are other churches who can't pay their bills. How can we be God's church and operate like that?"

96

Albert was already asking the hard questions about God's economic plan, even though he wasn't living that in his own life at the time. He knew that if the church was really God's business, it wouldn't need big cash reserves. When the church leaders said they needed a "rainy day fund," Albert mocked them.

Albert then became a Christian. He wanted to become a true follower of Christ and he was angry about what the church was doing. Finally, he convinced them to trust God by dispensing with the building fund collection and turning it into a mission related offering. The income of the church tripled over that next year and Albert believed it was because they were giving away their money--it was God's money all along.

"There's nothing wrong with savings," says Albert, "but don't rely on it. There are billions of dollars in reserve in Christian foundations. What if Christ came back today? What would we tell him? 'Lord, we were saving for a rainy day?'"

Albert never said endowments were wrong, but that he wasn't going to live that way. He saw himself as a lender of God's money to others; a lender who typically never intended to be repaid. "I believe the blessings talked about in the Bible related to being lenders applies to us whether we are ever repaid or not. I want to be a channel that God knows will flow out to wherever He wants it."

Selling God's Business

When Albert sold his business, he received a large lump sum as part of the transaction as well as the promise of twenty years of regular payments. Rather than building up his net worth or planning his retirement, he was compelled to put most of the lump sum into charities he had been supporting for years. He knew he wouldn't have the income level to support them at such a high level without his business and he wanted to be certain they were taken care of.

After a time, the business Albert had sold began to struggle. When the promised payments stopped, and Albert could not support himself, it would have been easy to ask God, WHY? Albert reasoned that he had not given intending to leverage God to bless him. He knew that whatever God was doing, it was for his good, even if he couldn't understand it. Albert was holding a promissory note for the remaining value and suddenly it seemed like an idol standing in front of God's provision for his life. Albert did the only thing he knew he could do that would release him from anything that would keep him from depending completely on God. He sent the promissory note back to the borrower and told him that if he were unable to pay, Albert would forgive the debt.

Albert had become both a giver and a lender. He had lived out the process of both within the knowledge that all provision comes from the hand of God and not from our own devices. The freedom Albert felt in releasing that burden became another step in placing all trust in God's hands. It was painful, and he didn't have the answer, but he knew God had a plan. He wasn't going to change his belief in God and he wasn't going to doubt.

To this day, God continues to provide for Albert, even when it seems invisible. Even when there seems to be no answer, Albert has learned to be patient and confident while God does what God does.

"I put all of my trust in Him so I know that it's not my problem. I can trust Him to take care of it."

Chapter 15 – What is Wealth, Anyway?

What is wealth? Albert postulates that only God knows what your wealth should be. He knows what is best for you. How do you handle these decisions when other people don't understand? When it doesn't seem right or humanly fair? When Albert said he wouldn't cosign on a loan that would clearly benefit his own business and had no discernable risk, he considered it a measure of the principles he believed in.

Even now, Albert says he feels scared when he comes to these decision points. Still, he knows what God has done in the past. He doesn't panic. He measures it against the principles he believes in. He accepts that in order for it to stay real, he must continue a process of learning, trusting, praying, studying and stepping out on faith.

"It isn't because we are so strong. It isn't because we are so good. God is the only one who is good, and He is good all the time. We just have to choose where we are going to put our trust. I trust in God."

Secretly, Albert admits he has always been afraid of being rich and trusting in those riches. Even before he was a Christian. He always wanted to help others. He didn't want to be a slave to money and he was brought up to be conservative financially. Even though this was true, however, his entire perspective of giving changed when he realized that God already owned everything. Since, whatever God already owned was His, GIVING wasn't really giving at all because it was already God's.

God was giving it to him because God trusted him to give it to others.

Most Christians say, "Yes, God owns it all," but that's not how they live. Albert was determined to find out the depth and height of God's plan for living a life completely dependent on Him.

At one point, Albert was driving his Oldsmobile thinking about this concept. God owns the earth and all that's on it. He thought about his ownership in that Oldsmobile. Suddenly he realized, *I don't own anything. When I die, it will all stay right here.*

We act like we own things, even though as Christians we intellectually know the difference. Guess what? If we practice it, we can really find out what it means to be free. Until we practice God's ownership of all our possessions, we will be a slave to them and to money.

Strangely enough, we want God to take over things only when they get bad. The reality is that true peace comes when we let go to God's ownership, good times or bad. How God deals with things is different with each one of us. That's not up to us.

Living in complete peace and satisfaction comes not from defining how God chooses to use us or to test us. It comes from resting in the blessings of God's presence and God's ownership in our lives.

The Freedom of Forgiveness

It's impossible for most business leaders to imagine the counterintuitive result of forgiveness. We spend our lives and our business energies keeping score. We keep track of everything that denotes what we owe and who owes us. We have expectations that help us to balance the proverbial books whether they are actual financial issues or not.

When Albert forgave the debt on the sale of his business, much as when he refused to sue after his unnecessary lung surgery, his business friends thought he was crazy. They could not understand. But what they did understand is that Albert was different. Albert was a Christian who really trusted God and it wasn't about the money. They may never have experienced this for themselves but the witness of God in their lives was seen through Albert and his consistency even in impossible and traumatic circumstances. They knew it was real.

"One of the biggest dangers of these challenging times as Christian Business leaders comes when we begin to buy into our own excuses," Albert explains.

"You have to start by giving up your own rights and confessing your desire to obey God. You have to believe that He will let you know what to do. If you do it, you will never regret it.

"So many people live with a constant sparring going on with God. They may even do the same with their spouse. They believe, somehow, they must negotiate to get something for themselves in the process of pleasing the other. They never just let go. Yes, we are sinful people. We can't trust ourselves at times, but we can trust God."

Chapter 16 – Cascading the Witness

CBMCI leaders in Brisbane, Australia during CBMCI world convention, 1992.

Through Albert's experience with CBMC, he learned the need for business leaders to connect with other Christian business leaders. Their circumstances and their challenges were unique. Soon CBMC asked him to run the state CBMC operations board. He was then chosen to be on the national board. In the process, he met a gentleman who had gone to Europe representing CBMC and found that they had been working with Holland. He told Albert that if he were ever back in Holland, he should contact them.

After Albert's surgery, he told his relatives in Holland that everything was fine, but they didn't seem to believe him. Finally, he decided he'd go to visit his home country. In May of 1981 he went to Holland

and decided he would indeed make connection with the CBMC contingency there. One evening he met with six of them. They had three CBMC groups in the Netherlands, but they functioned more like men's groups and didn't do the discipleship portion of CBMC anymore. Albert began pushing that they needed to begin doing discipleship. They discussed joining another group in Switzerland that was doing something similar, but they agreed that if Albert would commit the effort they would build CBMC in the Netherlands.

They insisted that Albert return and do a retreat for them in Dutch. He had never done a seminar or spoken in public, but he agreed. They listened to Albert and he became a credible leader. He laid out the way it was being done in the US, praying by name for other business men whom they believed were lost. Then, he listened to people give testimony of what God was doing in their lives and their businesses. They liked the concept and began routinely doing it in Holland.

God continued to bless Albert in business, so he was able to afford to pay his own expenses and return three times a year. Albert never wanted anyone else to pay his way, nor did he want to receive any personal benefit for his position at CBMC. He believed that if God wanted him to continue, God would provide the resources. He continued to lead, and they grew to more than a hundred groups.

On one trip, they asked if when he was next in Holland he would go to Portugal. He did. They finally hired a part-time leader who eventually became full-time to run the organization there. For a time, Albert paid for it all, 100%, from the blessings God was pouring on his business. God honored Albert's sacrifice, and from there it spread to many other countries.

Albert's One Condition

Albert shared: I told God, "I want to go wherever you want me to go, but I don't ever want to have to ask for support." Albert was constantly raising money for others in ministry, but he believed God would provide through his business.

"Business people have the opportunity to demonstrate God's ownership in their businesses, and their support for ministry through them."

Albert spoke and lived it with determination. "There is no separation between church and business. We are all ambassadors. God owns the business and Christ is the head of the church. The sphere of influence operating in God's principles is *one* with God and the church. This is true impact and influence. This is my role in the Kingdom."

"So, you want to get connected with what God is doing and with His Kingdom. It is the giving and the genuine leading of God that makes long-term connection and networking happen! What you can touch isn't going to be around for long. How can we touch our value? Our intellect? Our contribution to others? Our service?"

A friend in Austria told Albert something he would never forget. He learned from the fundamentalists to love the Bible. He learned from the charismatics how much God loves us. He learned from the Americans how to evangelize, but he learned from radical extremists the sense of urgency. "We, as Christians, don't have enough sense of urgency in sharing the Gospel."

Albert thought it would be cool to start a company and give away all of the proceeds. They formed the company and called it Ideal Computers. They gave away over $500,000 dollars as well as many computers. Albert realized that when people became united in a cause for God's Kingdom, not only will the results be amazing, but it can be a lot of fun.

The Kingdom of God

Albert was fascinated with all Jesus stories; about what the Kingdom of God was like. He noticed that Jesus never referred to what people had in the bank. His stories were most often about business men and managers, and how they dealt with their wealth, but also their talents. The story of the talents became the ultimate story of how God expected us to live. Albert could see what God's Kingdom looked like "on earth as it is in Heaven."

Albert never believed he was a good speaker and struggled when asked to speak. Still, he knew it was not just his bank account that God would use. His words and every other physical capability were totally committed to God.

Often it was easier to write a check than it was to make the personal sacrifice of answering the call.

Talents, just like everything else, are all about giving. We agree with what the Bible teaching says and then we apply it. Is it really God's money? God's time? God's business? Is it really God's principle or is it ours?

If we interpret God's principles based on our circumstances, we are destined to fail.

Albert knew that the Kingdom of God was not built on failure but upon the limitless resources of God. He continued teaching and spreading the word to everyone who would listen. Albert's business was his ministry. God used his abilities, his resources and his influence to fulfill the great commission.

Chapter 17 – Circumstance vs. Commitment

After a very successful business year, Albert's accountant advised him to spend money to reduce his taxes. Albert really wanted a used Mercedes, but the profit being discussed had already been given to others. His accountant told him he really needed to spend the money and that it would be easy to borrow, but Albert stood firm. "No, I said I would pay cash and I am not going to buy it unless I can."

That very day, unexpected money came in the mail from a new sale that was being pre-paid. It was more than enough to purchase the used car. Albert was tested, and he stood firm. Albert smiles now, knowing that God had it planned all along. It wasn't about the car. It was about the commitment he had made.

The Open Hand Theory

Albert reasoned,

> *"We make plans for what the future holds when we should be making plans based on God's ownership of our business, and not our right to do what we want with it."*

Albert believed in building his business with the Open Hand Theory. Give me today my daily bread. Let God put it in and take it out.

"There is nothing wrong with being rich as long as we are making decisions based on what God does with us individually. What gives God the Glory?"

Don't fail to plan. Decisions ahead of time are critical to taking appropriate actions. When you plan you are making decisions "in advance." You make decisions when the pressure is not what you are responding to. When you plan properly, you can make decisions based on principles you know are important. Having a life plan allows you to be prepared when the crisis decisions come.

And they will come.

If the underlying desire is riches, the love of money will be the root of all evil (I Timothy 6:9-10). We absolutely need to make a profit, but what is your motive? God says our motive should be *love*. Ecclesiastes 5:10 reminds us that "He who loves money will NOT be satisfied with money."

If you want to be satisfied with money, never fall in love with it.

If wealth is your purpose you will *never* be satisfied. It's a treadmill you can never get off.

What Are You Seeking?

"Do you really want satisfaction, or do you want money?" Albert asks a business gathering. "Let me pose a question. Do you believe that Matthew 6:33 is the truth? It says, 'seek first the Kingdom of God and His righteousness and all these things will be added unto you.' So, if you believe this Scripture, let me ask you a question. Which of these things will you give up if you pursue money? Family? Satisfaction? Peace? Contentment? If you choose to pursue money you won't get *any* of these things."

If we choose certain priorities, we will abandon others. It's that simple. If we choose to pursue riches, more possessions and stockpiled wealth, who will get the credit? What is the outcome for the resources generated by my life? Those were questions that drove Albert to action, teaching and asking others to embrace the greatest questions of their own lives and businesses.

"The enemy searches for our weak points as entry into our lives. Do you think his goal is to help us, or to destroy us? Do you think achieving human wisdom or worldly economic wisdom glorifies God? Is it wisdom, or is it a road to deny us what God promised us? If we make that exchange, then we really lose. As business leaders we *must* truly comprehend the exchange we are making."

For Albert, economic circumstances were defined in only one way. They were attacks of the enemy which attempt to dilute and deny us what God has offered and promised. He views our decisions as tests. They are truly opportunities when we can prove God's glory and when we can be faithful. The choice is ours and the opportunity is always before us.

"Every decision you make is a spiritual decision." (Larry Burkett)

Knowing God's Will

Let's be real. Sometimes we just don't know what God's plan is. but we can still know His will. His will is for us to trust him completely. His will is for us to thank and praise Him when we don't have evidence of what He will do. In fact, most of the time, we simply *don't know* what God's plan is or how He will deliver.

Albert maintains that *timing* is huge evidence of God's will and providence. God's timing vs ours. He has designed the necessity for us to *wait*. We *need* to wait. We need to listen. Faith is the evidence of things not seen. God gives us a chance to have faith in Him long before we have the evidence of what He is doing. If we believe only in outcomes that we can define, we will never include God's principles in our planning.

Albert was trying to live out God's principles in his business, and still it required daily discipline and reminder. Ownership of any idea changes when we hear ourselves speaking it. It's true in every area of our lives. If you want to experience the truth, you need to teach it. It's true of every principle God intended us to live by. It's even more true in business where God's economics often seem counterintuitive to the self-centered business logic of the world. For Albert, knowing God's will became a function of immersing himself in the known biblical principles God designed for the business leader. He knew he would be tested and that he wouldn't always understand, but he also knew without question that *this* was God's will.

Albert consistently suggested that business leaders should search out their decisions based on the following truths:

1. If you can't control what you already have, you don't need any more. I Timothy 6:6: "Godliness is great gain when it is accompanied by contentment."

2. If you want contentment, you need to determine what God would have your lifestyle to be. It's not about being poor or rich, it's about determining God's plan for your life.

3. Ask God to show you what your portion is. What should be the size of your business? Bigger is not necessarily a default decision in the economics of the Kingdom.

4. If we cannot maintain our priorities in God's Kingdom, we should not grow.

5. We must not grow our business beyond our ability to support that growth. If we violate a business principle in order to grow, we exceed the support for our growth and begin to rely on our own understanding.

6. If we find ourselves anxious and pushing for specific outcomes, we are not following God, we are trying to lead.

7. If you are diligent about pleasing God, God will take care of the results.

8. We don't want to get what God didn't plan for us to have.

9. Without accountability there will be no success. Hold yourself accountable to God's principles.

10. John 17 is the real Lord's prayer. "I have brought you glory on earth by finishing the work you gave me to do."

There can be no success where there is no eternal mission. Make a choice. Walk a path. Be certain you are walking a path that leads to your eternal reward.

Chapter 18 – Beyond Your Imagination

There is no question that when you follow God without holding back, you will experience things that exceed your wildest imagination. Albert has come face-to-face with this many times in his efforts to be faithful in sharing business principles with Christian leaders across the globe.

Albert helped organize training on cruise ships with Chuck Colson, Jack Kemp and Alistair Begg. Every time it happened, Albert felt out of place, odd to be part of such powerful worldwide ministries. God had other ideas. Albert was determined that the message he had been ordained to speak would be heard.

Albert with Jack Kemp and Prison Fellowship Tour in Jerusalem.

Albert with Chuck and Patty Colson in Rothenberg, Germany
at the CBMCI World convention, 1996.

He participated with Chuck Colson in the national prayer breakfasts, and through those experiences met many powerful Christian leaders. He met Jim Dobson and Robert Schuller in the height of their careers of ministry. They weren't perfect men, but Albert felt their passion and the momentum of God using them. How did he get to be involved in these situations?

Albert coined a phrase that he continues to use to this day:

"I believe God has you right where he wants you."

For Albert, that meant saying yes to whatever he believed God was asking him to do.

It's amazing how consistently God allows challenge and struggle to enter the picture. Attacks that became opportunities to prove Albert's love for the Father and to keep his faith rooted in Him for strength. On one occasion Albert was representing CBM. Albert was on the board of CBMC International for some 16 years, Chairman for eight years. A group of Koreans living in Chicago came together to establish a chapter of CBMC. They asked Albert to speak to them. More than 250 Christian Korean businessmen came for the event. They flew in powerful political figures to participate from South Korea.

President of Ideal Computer Services – Albert's store in Kankakee, 1990.

Albert became sick and in such severe pain that he feared he would not even be able to speak. He had planned to travel home that night after the event, but arrangements had been made for him to have breakfast with a member of the South Korean Parliament. This man would later become the President of South Korea. Knowing the significance of this, Albert agreed to stay until morning. In the night his pain became so severe that he was rushed to the emergency room, only to discover that his colon had ruptured, and he was literally on the verge of death.

Being driven to the hospital by his son-in-law, Albert passed out several times from the pain. In a struggling conscious state, Albert fell back on the most important truth of his life. "Thank you, Lord, even in this circumstance. I don't know what is happening, but I trust you." Those were the words of faith and experience with his loving Father that Albert relied on in good times and in bad.

CBMC - Taiwan national convention.

Self-Sufficiency

How can you separate the essential elements of an effective life and business from the temptation of self-sufficiency and the platform that is built from it?

That was a common merger Albert spoke of when businessmen were searching for the truth. Albert always explained that the same question is true in every area of our lives and it always starts with giving. Everything has a flipside. We want to show what God can do and what God has done, but there is danger in drawing attention to the fact that you are the one in the middle who is doing it. How can you do both?

How can you teach and exhibit God's evidence of abundance, and still remain surrendered and without any form of self-sufficiency?

How do you tell people the wonderful things God is doing and how much you trust him without bringing attention to yourself in the process? Somehow, according to Albert, you can't let your right hand know what your left hand is doing. You can't boast that you are a generous giver. It's all God's anyway. How can you acknowledge both?

It's often a paradox and it can be a dangerous shift in our thinking, warns Albert. The truth is simple. If we are one with Christ, we are going to have moments of influence that we don't expect. We are going to have exponential results that have nothing to do with our own efforts other than our effort to glorify God. We must subordinate our influence to the *process of Christ.*

We *only* boast in Christ.

We remain constantly vulnerable, and in that vulnerability we will be tested by pride and legitimate sounding praise. We are blessed by the opportunity to give praise where it is due and to participate in the process of Christ as he taught us to glorify our Father God in Heaven. With this as our focus, we will live a life beyond our greatest imagination, witnessing the presence of God "on earth as it is in Heaven."

Chapter 19 – Knowing Albert

Spending time with Albert, I have benefitted from a wealth of overflow. I must share some of the many things you would hear Albert say if you were lucky like I have been. I know you'll treasure these words as much as I do. Some are his own quotes, and some absorbed from the many inspiring leaders he has known, but all of them are based in scripture, for faith comes by hearing the word of Christ (Romans 10:17).

For this book to have any value in Albert's legacy, it must speak the message and continue the calling to biblical principles which have manifest themselves in Albert through painful lessons. These words are the culmination of those truths.

My Favorite Albert Expressions:

I couldn't resist adding this section to share my favorite Albert-isms. At the risk of redundancy, I am consolidating them here for easy reference. Those of you who know Albert will hear his voice in them (as an emissary), but every word is based in scripture and intended to bring glory to God.

"People get hung up so much on doctrine, especially the doctrine they have grown up with. After a while that matters less to me. I don't need to be right. I need to stay inside God's will and follow what I know he has told us. The rest just works out."

"God gave us the Holy Spirit. We can trust the intuition of the Spirit. We won't always know logically, in fact we may argue with ourselves about it logically, but we need to trust the Spirit and trust that He will openly guide our spirit."

"God's Spirit is like an unseen partner in our lives and our business. The advisor that we know and trust, but sometimes fail to give full attention to. He's always there and sometimes causes us to feel uneasy. We don't know why we feel this way, but we do. It is part of his intervention in our lives. We can trust it." (Proverbs 3:5-6)

"The world is never in step with God. Making sense business-wise sometimes won't be in step with the principles of God. You have to stick with God's principles whether it seems to make sense in that moment or not."

"If you find yourself arguing with how to interpret what God has said, it's because you want to fit it into your own needs and your own logic. Even that should tell you what you need to do."

"People have the tendency to always try to build themselves up in whatever they do, but that's not what we are called to do. If we are managing God's business, we don't need to rely on the opinions of others."

"Business owners don't like accountability and that's the biggest reason we all need it."

"God will only reveal his plan through someone who is willing to do it."

"God can direct by supplying or by withholding money. Most Christians will accept His supply but start borrowing when He withholds. *If you want to know what God is up to, you have to wait on Him to show up.*"

"When you decide to live by God's principles you won't normally fit into the society we are living in."

"The prerequisites for trust are knowing God's Word, acknowledging God's authority, accepting God's direction and accepting our responsibility."

"Money and wealth are tools for doing God's work. Nothing else. We only manage God's resources." (2 Chronicles 29)

"If we are ethical it is because our practices are motivated by principle rather than by profit."

"The church and the business should be in the world but not of the world. A ship doesn't sink because it gets into the water, it sinks when the water gets into the ship."

"When you accept one of God's principles, you are going to be challenged on it. YOU WILL BE. Believe it."

"We can always justify our own actions, but it isn't about justifying them. It's about listening to God's plan."

"We can justify saving for the future based on taking care of our children, but the reality is that we can't take care of them. Only God can take care of them. They will model what they see in our lives. They need to see us put our trust completely in God."

"Somewhere along the way we got confused with the difference between simple and easy. God's principles are simple, but I never said they were easy."

"If you stay obedient, the outcome is not your problem."

"Don't fail to realize that the economic engine of Heaven is the one we can use here as well. If we aren't progressing on a path that can be continuous in Heaven, then we better question our path. We should be able to step right into Heaven with the same principles we are using today."

"Don't make promises easily. Promises will always be tested. When you make them, be ready to do whatever is required to live up to them. Now go out and make some promises to God and watch what happens."

"There is a deep connection between God's promises to us and our promises to Him."

"If you want to go farther in business than you ever imagined, make some promises to God based on His principles."

"It's not about us. It is about God fulfilling His promises. Even Job went through hell, but it was to glorify God. That's the purpose of our lives and our businesses."

"God will never give you a principle that you cannot implement."

"If you never really trust, you can never learn or experience the result of that trust."

"A loving father will never let something happen to me that is not for my good. I can trust Him. I may not feel thankful, but I can be thankful because I know I can trust him."

"I told God I wasn't going to borrow money ever again and I wasn't going to go back on my word."

"If you are on the wrong track but you really want God's will, you will know it."

"What if Christ came back today? What would we tell him? 'Lord, we were saving for a rainy day?'"

"I believe the blessings talked about in the Bible related to being lenders applies to us whether we are ever repaid or not. I want to be a channel that God knows will flow out to wherever He wants it."

"I put all of my trust in Him, so I know that it's not my problem. I can trust Him to take care of it."

"It isn't because we are so strong. It isn't because we are so good. God is the only one who is good, and He is good all the time. We just have to choose where we are going to put our trust. I trust in God."

"I don't own anything. When I die it will all stay right here."

"Until we practice God's ownership of all our possessions, we will be a slave to them and to money."

"One of the biggest dangers of these challenging times as Christian business leaders comes when we begin to buy into our own excuses."

"You have to start by giving up your own rights and confessing your desire to obey God. You have to believe that He will let you know what to do and if you do it, you will never regret it."

"So many people live with a constant sparring between them and God. They may even do the same with their spouse. They believe, somehow, that they must negotiate to get something for themselves in the process of pleasing the other. They never just let go. Yes, we are sinful people. We can't trust ourselves at times, but we can trust God."

"Business people have the opportunity to demonstrate God's ownership in their businesses and their support for ministry through them."

"There is no separation between church and business. We are all ambassadors. God owns the business and Christ is the head of the church. The sphere of influence operating in God's principles is *one* with God and the church. This is true impact and influence. This is my role in the Kingdom."

"Get connected with what God is doing and with His Kingdom people. What you can touch isn't going to be around for long."

"Get involved in a cause for God's Kingdom. Not only will the results be amazing, but it will be a lot of fun."

"If we interpret God's principles based on our circumstances, we are destined to fail."

"We make plans for what the future holds when we should be making plans based on God's ownership of our business and not our right to do what we want with it."

"If you want to be satisfied with money, never fall in love with it."

"If we choose certain priorities, we will abandon others. It's that simple."

"Our decisions are tests. They are truly opportunities when we can prove God's glory and when we can be faithful. The choice is ours and the opportunity is always before us."

"If you want to experience the truth, you need to teach it."

"If you can't control what you already have, you don't need any more. I Timothy 6:6: "Godliness is great gain when it is accompanied by contentment."

"If you want contentment, you need to determine what God would have your lifestyle be. It's not about being poor or rich, it's about determining God's plan for your life."

"If we cannot maintain our priorities in God's Kingdom, we should not grow."

"We must not grow our business beyond our ability to support that growth. If we violate a business principle in order to grow, we exceed the support for our growth and begin to rely on our own understanding."

"If we find ourselves anxious and pushing for specific outcomes, we are not following God, we are trying to lead."

"If you are diligent about pleasing God, God will take care of the results."

"We don't want to get what God didn't plan for us to have."

"Without accountability there will be no success. Hold yourself accountable to God's principles."

"There can be no success where there is no eternal mission. Make a choice. Walk a path. Be certain you are walking a path that leads to your eternal reward."

"I believe God has you right where he wants you." (This is my personal favorite.)

"If we are one with Christ, we are going to have moments of influence that we don't expect. We are going to have exponential results that have nothing to do with our own efforts other than our effort to glorify God. Always remember, we must only boast in Christ."

Chapter 20 – Biblical Principles

Throughout this book we've talked about the biblical principles for business. The only thing Albert insisted on in this book is that we talk about these principles and give God the glory.

If you're reading this, please know one thing above everything else. Albert is allowing his story to be told so that you (yes, you) will come to believe as a result. Don't be afraid. You can trust God, just like Albert has. You can experience a life of peace and God's favor beyond your imagination if you follow these simple principles.

This is intended for the Christian business leader, more than anyone else, but God's truth is always faithful. If you don't understand, ask for understanding. If you are afraid, read about fear in God's Word. Fear only comes from placing our trust in something besides God.

If God is for us, who can be against us?

I challenge you to apply these truths in your life and your business. You can become a person after God's own heart when you trust completely in Him. This isn't about separating business and faith. If you have faith in God, you literally have an unfair advantage in business when you follow God's business principles.

Welcome to the greatest opportunity of your life.

Here's what you need to know (and the scriptures where you can learn more):

1. God created everything. God owns everything, and we are only trustees. (Genesis 1:1, Haggai 2:8, Psalm 50:10, Psalm 37:21)

2. We can't serve two masters. You can't serve both God and money. If your 'stuff' gets between you and God, it definitely is master over you. (1 Corinthians 4:1-2, Matthew 6:24)

3. We are supposed to pursue biblical knowledge about business and money. There are a lot of misconceptions. You need to pursue this knowledge for yourself. (Proverbs 15:22, Proverbs 23:23)

4. Our plans should be committed to the Lord before we can expect them to succeed. (Proverbs 16:3)

5. Being trustworthy matters. God won't trust us with much until we prove we can be trusted with little. (Luke 16: 10-12)

6. Work is from God. (Colossians 3:23)

7. We are supposed to care for those entrusted to us; our family and our employees. (1 Timothy 5:8)

8. Remember that everything comes from God and be thankful. (Deuteronomy 8:18)

9. Enjoy your work and be content in it. It is a gift from God. (Ecclesiastes 5: 18-19)

10. Earn through honest work and share the excess. Give to everyone in need. (Ephesians 4:28)

11. God expects us to give to others as He has given to us. Everything we have is His. True freedom comes in living with the open hand. Giving is worship. (James 1:17)

12. Give to break the hold of money on your life. (Matthew 6:33, 2 Corinthians 8: 13-14, Genesis 12: 2-3, 1 Timothy 6:18)

13. Give wisely, expectantly and cheerfully. (2 Cor: 8: 1-5, 2 Cor 9: 6-7)

14. Examine your motives. (Matthew 23:23)

15. It's wise to save but it's sinful to hoard. (Proverbs 21:20, Proverbs 6:8, Luke 12: 16-21)

16. Count the cost. Prioritize. Set a budget. (Luke 14: 28-30)

17. Avoid "get rich" schemes. God's riches come through a process of sowing and reaping. (Proverbs 28:20)

18. Seek wise counselors. (Proverbs 1:5)

19. Diversify your holdings. (Ecclesiastes 11:2)

20. Be a cautious debtor. (Luke 12:22-32, Ecclesiastes 7:14)

21. Repay debt promptly. (Ps 37:21, Proverbs 3:28)

22. Avoid the bondage of debt. Remember that debt presumes on the future. (Proverbs 22:7)

23. Debt can deny God the opportunity to work in our lives and teach us valuable lessons. (Ecclesiastes 7:14, Luke 12: 22-32)

24. Debt can foster envy and greed. (Luke 12:5)

25. Don't cosign or guarantee anyone else's loan. (Proverbs 22: 26-27)

26. Debt can disrupt spiritual growth. (Galatians 5: 22-23)

27. Beware of idols - materialism is the greatest idol. (Deuteronomy 5:8, Romans 1:25)

28. Guard against greed because it does not bring happiness. (Luke 12: 15)

29. Seek moderation. Give me neither poverty nor riches but give me only my daily bread. Otherwise, I may have too much and disown you and say, 'Who is this Lord?' I may become poor and steal, and so dishonor the name of my God. (Proverbs 30: 8-9)

30. Be content in every situation. (Philippians 4: 12-13, 1 Timothy 6:6-8)

31. Don't waste God's resources. (John 6:12)

32. Enjoy a portion of God's provision but lay up for yourself treasures in Heaven. (1 Timothy 6: 17-19)

33. Watch your finances. Budget. (Proverbs 27: 23-24)

Chapter 21 – The Takeaway

Worshipping happens in many different ways. True worship is in living a life that brings honor to God. True worship not only talks about His deity but depends on it with complete faith and actions of trust. Faith without work is dead.

As painful as it is for us to separate ourselves from our identity, God asks us as business leaders to place our identity squarely in Him. He defines the path and then promises to manifest himself in it if we'll just trust him. I love the story of Albert's life, not just because he was powerful, or successful, or because of the influence he carries so easily to this day. All of this is true, but I love the story for a different reason. It is the story of a man who made a simple decision to trust God and still sees the decision as clearly as when he started.

If you know Albert, you know how desperately he wants to downplay himself and how passionate he is to talk about the life of complete fulfillment he has experienced. For Albert, it's mind-boggling to imagine why any Christian would miss out on this adventure.

So, what is the takeaway? What is the message for the Christian business leader? If you're like me, I initially saw Albert as an anomaly; the exception to the rule. I mean, let's face it, we're not blatantly ignoring God or robbing him, are we? Isn't it our own decision to make? Aren't we entitled to varying "degrees" of service?

Nobody can answer that question except you. Nobody can draw you closer to God, or experience for you the intimacy or the contractual relationship you may choose to have. I do know this. You were created for intimacy with God.

You have been given opportunity to reach beyond your own logic and the limitations of this world, into the reservoir of possibilities that only exist in God.

It's scary. It's risky. It doesn't have a playbook that demonstrates clear expectation that you can monitor. It opens possibilities outside your control and gives you a chance to say "yes."

"But store up for yourselves treasures in Heaven where moths and vermin do not destroy and where thieves do not break in and steal. For where your treasure is, there your heart will be also."

(Matthew 6: 20-21 NIV)

I suppose we all want preference, but in this case, preference doesn't bring Glory to God. "Choose you this day whom you will serve." Choose now who you will honor, trust, and yes, serve. When it comes down to it, everything you're dreaming for will be found when you receive the promises made by our true Father and Sovereign King.

It won't be easy, but let's face it, you didn't go into business because it was easy. You were born to fight. Now it's time to be sure you're fighting the right fight. Don't let the distractions of this life, the cares of life and the pursuit of wealth (parable of the sower), become the legacy you trade for.

Thank you, Albert, for showing us that it can be done and calling us to live by the timeless principles of God's Word. Thank you for your mentorship, your leadership and your legacy of faith in God's principles.

Thank you for your story, Albert. We're only beginning to imagine what *true* legacy looks like. A Journey of Significance.

"The King will reply, 'truly I tell you, whatever you did for the least one of these brothers and sisters of mine, you for me.'" *Matthew 25:40.*

About the Author

Greg Yates is a Chicago area businessman writing from firsthand experience about extreme business success and failure. Greg's unique experiences in both corporate boardrooms and federal prison enable him to share the message of Christian businesses struggles with the implementation of timeless biblical principles.

Greg's humbling admission, *Broken*, is the testimonial foundation as Greg pursues the calling to awaken and equip Christian businessmen.

Is there a balance for Christians? How can we integrate ancient methodology into a process already moving at the speed of business? Is there really an actionable place for faith in my business? Can God really bring security when I don't have the answers? Are my struggles representative of a lack of faith, or the presence of sin in my life?

How can I get God on my timetable?

What is the *true purpose* of my life and my business?

Can God still use me after I have failed?

If you're engaged in the genuine struggle to honor God and survive in a world that almost never gets it right, download Greg's latest eBook for free: *Overcoming 10 Common Leadership FEARS: How to Turn Common Fear into Your Uncommon Breakthrough.*

Greg writes and speaks to the Christian business leader who is willing to ask the most important questions of life and business. As a business leader, you're on a journey--and you don't need to do it alone.

You can follow Greg through his blog, podcast, and future writing at morethanbreakthrough.com. Greg is also available for business events and seminars on a variety of topics, including his personal journey from wealth to prison and back to wholeness. For speaking engagements and all other inquiries, please contact Greg at greg@morethanbreakthrough.com.

Acknowledgements

Thank you, Albert, for sitting with me countless hours answering my questions. For inspiring me each time with the resonance of your experience and firmness of your convictions. I know you didn't want this book to be written *about you*, but you accepted my belief that these stories will make a lasting impact on others and bring honor to God.

Thank you, Albert, Theresa, Ineke, and Annette for your encouragement and patience in this process. I've been deeply honored to share in the intimacy of your family relationship.

Made in the USA
Middletown, DE
16 November 2018